Valuing Diversity and Similarity:
Bridging the Gap through Interpersonal Skills

by

Joe Wittmer, Ph.D.

Contributors:

Antonio Avila, Ph.D.
Chikako Inoue-Cox, Ph.D.
Diane Estrada, Ed.S.
Mary Fukuyama, Ph.D.
Saundra Henderson, Ed.S.
Carlos Hernandez, Ed.S.
Mary Howard-Hamilton, Ed.D.
Eugia Littlejohn, Ed.S.
Patricia Reifel, M.Ed.

D0112102

Copyright 1992
Educational Media Corporation®
P.O. Box 21311
Minneapolis, MN 55421-0311
1 (612) 781-0088

Library of Congress Catalog Card No. 92-071010

ISBN 0-932796-37-0

Printing (Last Digit)

9 8 7 6 5 4 3

Production editor—
Don L. Sorenson, Ph.D.

Graphic design—
Earl Sorenson

Joe Wittmer, Ph.D.

Dedication

This book is dedicated to my granddaughters, Raechel Diane and Haley Elaine Thompson. May they grow to appreciate diversity.

The Author:

Joe Wittmer, Ph.D., is Professor of Counselor Education at the University of Florida, Gainesville.

Dr. Wittmer has written more than 75 referred journal articles and has authored or co-authored several books. His three latest books are: *Experiencing and Counseling Multicultural and Diverse Populations* (Co-author, 1988); *The Teacher as Facilitator* (Co-author, 1989) and *The Gentle People: Personal Reflections on Amish Life* (1990). The latter book is based on Dr. Wittmer's cultural background. He was born and reared for sixteen years in the horse-and-buggy, German speaking Old Order Amish faith and is Vice-Chair of the *National Committee for Amish Religious Freedom*. His committee initiated, and won, the Supreme Court decision exempting the Amish from compulsory education laws.

References and Acknowledgments:

A very special thanks to Drs. Larry Loesch and Robert Myrick, colleagues, for their assistance with this manuscript. In addition, a very special thanks is extended to Antonio Avila, Ph.D.; Chikako Inoue-Cox, Ph.D.; Diane Estrada, Ed.S.; Mary Fukuyama, Ph.D.; Suandra Henderson, Ed.S.; Carlos Hernandez, Ed.S.; Mary Howard-Hamilton, Ed.D.; Eugia Littlejohn, Ed.S.; and Patricia Reifel, M.Ed. for their respective, special contributions to this book. Appreciation is also extended to Candy Spires and Judy Garis for their help in typing.

Every effort has been made to give proper acknowledgment to all those who have contributed to this book. Any omissions or errors are regretted and, upon notification, will be corrected in subsequent editions.

Table of Contents

Preface

We admire and enjoy being with "facilitative communicators." They sense and respect uniqueness. They value and appreciate people for their differences and similarities. Facilitative communicators like to learn and have an interest in diverse perspectives.

We tend to be drawn to people who make us feel at ease when we talk with them. They show an interest in our ideas and respect our feelings. We may not realize what is happening at the moment, but we leave with favorable impressions. Sometimes we fail to recognize how skillful good communicators are in helping us to talk about ourselves and to hear what others are saying. Being a facilitative communicator is not necessarily a "gift" with which people are born. Rather, it involves skills that can be learned and an awareness and sensitivity toward others that can be developed. We can improve our working and personal relationships through better communication. As relationships improve, so does the quality of life.

This book is a step-by-step approach that will help you to develop the skills needed to be a careful listener and a more effective speaker (i.e., "communicator"). It can enhance your interactions. In particular, it outlines an approach and provides examples that can help you to facilitate communication among people with different cultural heritages. It is a manual to help you to relate more effectively with multi-cultural groups, focusing on the *what, why,* and *how* of facilitative communication.

To facilitate others means to "draw people out," to "enhance," or, as one of my students said, "to make it [talking] flow easily." When you communicate in facilitative ways, other people are comfortable talking with you. You help them think about their ideas and feelings. In the process, you will learn a lot about them.

The future of our society and nation is becoming increasingly more dependent on being able to communicate effectively with others, especially those of a different culture or sub-culture. Effective communication is the basis for improving relationships, understanding others, and appreciating diversity and similarity among people.

In today's society communication between and among multi-cultural groups is essential. It is an important skill, no matter if you are a White Anglo-American farmer in Nebraska, an African-American college student in Florida, a Native-American medical doctor in North Dakota, a female dentist in Iowa, a Mexican-American business leader in Texas, or an Asian-American salesperson in California. We are a nation of diverse populations and groups. The future of our society depends upon our ability to talk with one another and to reach mutual understanding. As we understand ourselves and others better, we gain more respect and personal regard. There are less fears and anxieties. Communication paves the way for tolerance and patience. It is the bases for caring and valuing.

Your interpersonal skills are valuable resources. To maximize your potential, and to make positive contributions to our nation and society, you must communicate effectively with others, regardless of race, culture, religion, or gender.

The term *intercultural communication* refers to an oral and nonverbal exchange of information between members of different cultural and racial groups. It is communication among persons who often share different patterns of thought and who may look at their individual worlds differently. Family heritage and culture have a major influence on peoples' attitudes, beliefs, values, opinions, and how they view others.

Intercultural communication skills might be conversations between Easterners and Westerners, Asians and Whites, Whites and Blacks, Asians and Blacks, Native Americans and Latinos. The skills can improve discourse between rich and poor, males and females, educated and uneducated, and so on. In short, inter-cultural communication results when interactions occur between members of different cultural and sub-cultural groups.

To develop effective communication skills, it is important for you to be aware of self and others. You must be willing to learn new ways of thinking about people, relationships, and communication skills. This book is divided into three sections. The science and art of communication is first addressed. In the second section attention is given to increasing your knowledge and understanding of multicultural communication, including some helpful insights concerning four different cultural groups. Individual thoughts and feelings—two characteristics common to all human beings—are fundamental elements in communication. However, your willingness to disclose thoughts and feelings stem from cultural backgrounds and personal experience, some of which may not always have encouraged open communication. While there are interpersonal and cultural barriers, this second section can help you to break through or reduce them. This section was written in collaboration with friends who are members of the culturally distinct groups of which they write. In the last section, the focus is on skills associated with facilitative communication. Finally, Dr. Mary Howard-Hamilton provides an insightful epilogue for the book based on professional and personal experience.

Besides providing knowledge and describing facilitative skills, study and practice activities are included in this book. Many of these activities can be completed individually. However, you probably will enjoy the book more (and learn more about yourself and others) if you complete the activities in sequence with others. A leader (e.g., an instructor or appointed group member) can lead and conduct the activities.

Activities such as those found at the end of each chapter are referenced when the origins of such exercises are known. However, they are often difficult to trace, having been passed on by word of mouth, on bits of paper, and on unsigned, undated mimeographed sheets.

Valuing diversity and appreciating similarities begins with understanding. It is always based on how open we are to learning about others and how aware we are of our own personal experiences when we are with them. Facilitating intercultural communication can be an adventure, one in which new friendships develop and personal insights occur. It can be fun. It can mean the difference between a society that is perplexing and troublesome and one that is positive and hopeful. By helping to facilitate others, you will invariably facilitate your own personal growth and self-esteem. You will learn to value your own diversity and similarity to others.

Joe Wittmer
March, 1992

Section I

The Science and Art of Communication

Chapter I

Communication: Connecting with Others

Chapter II
Behavior and Communication*

Chapter III
Nonverbal Behaviors and Communication

Chapter IV
Multicultural Communication

*Appreciation is extended to Drs. Robert Myrick and Don Sorenson for permission to quote and reprint from their book, *Peer Helping: A Practical Guide,* Minneapolis, MN., Educational Media Corporation, 1988.

Chapter *I*

Communication: Connecting with Others

We communicate in many ways and in many different situations. We interact with adults, children, students, teachers, friends, and even strangers with whom we may share only a few brief moments together. We are almost always communicating something to somebody.

The need and desire to communicate begins during our first weeks of life. As human beings, we cannot *not* communicate! We are always either saying or implying our ideas, attitudes, or feelings, even when we sit silently.

I see communication as a huge umbrella that covers and affects all that goes on between human beings. Once a human being arrives on this earth, communication is the largest single aspect determining what happens to him [her] in the world about him [her]. How one manages personal survival, develops intimacy, becomes productive, makes sense of life and connects with divinity are largely dependent on communication skills.

Virginia Satir

Why study interpersonal communication? Why study an activity that you have been doing all your life--one that seems so natural? Why? Because we can be better at communication.

There are skills that can be learned that will make us more effective communicators, both with those who are culturally similar or those who are culturally different.

Facilitative communication, which focuses on enhancing discussion among people, may not come naturally. It is achieved when skills are learned and applied.

Think for a moment about the time you spend interacting and talking with others. Many of our daily events involve communication with others. A recent study found that, when awake, we spend more than 60% of our time communicating "one on one" with another human being! Sometimes the experience can be exciting and invigorating, while at other times it may be wearisome and unpleasant.

Communication brings us into relationships with others. The evidence is clear, we need to interact with other humans and communication skills determine the outcomes of our interactions. Solitude is often a welcome relief, but most of us do not like much of it. Most people, regardless of cultural background, do not enjoy being alone for extended periods of time. We want to be with people, especially those who listen to us and encourage us to share our thoughts.

One of our greatest human needs is to believe that we are worthwhile and valued individuals. As human beings we seek confirmation about our worth from others. In this sense, we need to establish and maintain close relationships with other people. A basic human desire is to like and be liked by others, and to engage in communication with others. We want to give and receive love. We have a basic need for closeness and also a separateness that acknowledges our uniqueness and self-identity. These essential needs, regardless of our cultural background, cannot be satisfied without interpersonal communication.

Satisfying interpersonal relationships make us feel good about life and ourselves. Think back to a time when you had not seen a close friend for some time. When you saw the person, do you recall your experience? Did a pleasurable feeling of anticipation sweep across you? You may have been excited, knowing that, regardless of what would be discussed, you would feel renewed through an interesting exchange. The friendly relationship probably made the topic of discussion almost irrelevant, as you simply enjoyed being in the presence of someone you knew and cared about.

What is peculiarly characteristic of the human world is about all that something that takes place between one being and another the like of which can be found nowhere in nature.... It is rooted in one being turning to another as another, as this particular other being, in order to communicate with it in a sphere... the sphere of "between."

Martin Buber

How much do we need interpersonal communication with others? How important is it? Frederick II, Emperor of Germany during the twelfth century, developed an elaborate and chilling experiment with children. He wanted to see whether newborn infants would speak Hebrew, Greek, Latin, Arabic, or any other language if left alone. Using his power as King, he forbade mothers and nurses to play with, suckle, bathe, smile, or touch some children. Further, no interpersonal communication was permitted, as he was curious about what language would emerge. His misguided experiment was in vain because all of the children died! As the king learned, survival without touch and interpersonal communication is impossible.

A similar experiment with 200 babies was tried in a Nazi concentration camp in Germany under Adolf Hitler's regime. Half of them were assigned to adults, imprisoned women, as surrogate mothers. The mothers were instructed to feed the babies three times a day, but to have no other contact with them. The surrogate mothers were forbidden to talk with or touch the children. There was to be no eye contact with the children while feeding them. An additional 100 surrogate mothers were assigned to the other 100 children. These adults were instructed to spend as much time as possible with their foster children. They were to hold, cuddle, feed, and talk with them and to remain in close contact with the child personally assigned to them. The women also were told that if the baby assigned to them died, they too would be killed! Sadly, the results were the same as those for the Frederick II experiment. Those children left alone soon began dying until all passed away. The other children flourished (Podesta, 1989).

Research (e.g., Stewart, 1986) indicated that socially isolated people are two to three times more likely to die prematurely than are those with strong social ties. The kind or type of relationship does not seem to matter: marriage, friendship, and community ties all appear to add to longevity. Furthermore, divorced men (before age 70) die from heart disease, cancer, and strokes at almost double the rate of married men. Three times as many divorced as married men die from hypertension; 5 times as many commit suicide; 7 times as many die from cirrhosis of the liver; and 10 times as many die from tuberculosis. Stewart (1986) also noted that the rate of all types of cancer is as much as five times higher for divorced men and women, compared to their single counterparts.

Poor interpersonal communication also can contribute to coronary disease. One Swedish study examined 32 pairs of identical twins. One sibling in each pair had heart disease, whereas the other was healthy. The researchers found that smoking habits, cholesterol levels, and levels of obesity of the healthy and sick twins did not differ significantly. Among the significant differences, however, were "poor childhood and adult interpersonal relationships," the ability to resolve conflicts, and the degree of emotional support given by others in the group with heart disease (Stewart, 1986).

The likelihood of death increases when a close relative dies. In one Welsh village, citizens who had lost a close relative within one year died at a rate more than five times greater than those who had not suffered from a relative's death (Stewart, 1986).

Research supports our need for satisfying interpersonal relationships and it indicates that good interpersonal communication is important to our very survival! Communication and interpersonal relationships can influence life style and whether or not we live healthy lives.

Almost as important, interpersonal relationships and the communication that takes place in those relationships affect how we learn who we are and how we try to maintain our personal identities. Our personal identity is significantly influenced by the way in which we interact with others. People are complex and, likewise, so is the process of interpersonal communication.

Why Learn Communication Skills?

Some people may believe that good interpersonal communication is an innate aptitude, something that people are just naturally inclined to be able to do without training. They view communication as a part of being human and the process is inevitable, almost involuntary, like breathing. However, research indicates that most of us do not utilize our potential for communication and that our skill level is far below what it could be.

Communication skills can be learned. Just as you have learned to read or learned to play a game, you can learn communication skills. True, some people may have more aptitude for learning the skills, perhaps as those who have more aptitude in learning music or math, but the skills can be learned.

Even the most skilled musicians, for instance, struggled when they first began playing their instruments. They felt inept and at times they became frustrated, especially as they moved on to more complicated musical scores or techniques. The more accomplished musicians, of course, became proficient by increasing their knowledge and awareness, and by practicing certain skills over and over.

Communication is not easy. It is one of the most difficult things we ever accomplish. And the trouble is that it doesn't stop demanding something of us once we have broken through to the other—it requires constant effort. We ought to bear in mind always the alternative to communication—death. That's right. None of us is worth anything alone. We need other people. They are extensions of us. When we decide it isn't worth the trouble, we are saying we are not worth it. Marriages die. Corporations die. Individuals die.

John R. Killinger

You can learn to facilitate communication. Although some people may appear to be "naturally" talented and more inclined to be facilitative than others, you can be equally effective in many situations. Admittedly, some people have an advantage. They grew up in households where effective communication skills were modeled or they experienced teachers who consistently demonstrated skills that could be emulated. Yet, even these fortunate ones can likely improve their ability to communicate through the study and practice of facilitative skills.

Do you know someone who seems to be a natural athlete? Some athletes, because of heredity, past experiences, and encouragement, are able to perform in sports better than others. The most gifted athlete, however, can be assisted to become even better and to reach more potential through coaching and opportunities to study and integrate proven techniques, procedures, and strategies. How can you best capitalize on your strengths? The best coaches observe carefully and study behavior. They analyze actions and flow of the events. They make a few suggestions and encourage you to experiment with a new idea or skill. Improved performance is the goal and outcome determines if a new approach is to be added and practiced until it is fully integrated. Champions, of course, do not over intellectualize the process of performing. It could stifle their reactions and make them feel stiff and unresponsive. Likewise, champion communicators do not over analyze their relationships and skills, especially when they are trying to facilitate a conversation. Rather, they go with the flow of the events, using their best skills which they have learned and practiced. Later, they analyze their performance and think of ways which they might improve so that next time they can be more effective and the outcomes more rewarding.

Later in this book I will focus on some fundamental communication skills that will make a positive difference in your interpersonal relationships. They are skills that will be useful to you in all parts of your life with persons who are different and similar. Their use will also assist you in gaining an appreciation, awareness, sensitivity toward, and understanding of cultural diversity and sameness.

There will be times when you will want to improve your communication with someone, maybe someone from a different culture. Listening, responding selectively, and giving and receiving are part of the facilitative process. Each of these concepts are dealt with in more detail in later chapters.

Relationships and Communication

You experience many different kinds of human relationships. Some are casual and fleeting, others are deeply personal and involve commitment. The kind of relationships you have with other people usually determines the nature of the communications you have with them.

The most common type of relationships you have with others are *impersonal*. There are many people you know only by appearance. You have never talked with them, but you have seen them on occasion. You might recognize a neighbor down the street, someone who attends the same school, or a teacher who offers a class that you have not yet taken. These people may play a small role in your life and their impact on you seems minimal. They are much like figures in the background of a painting. They add to the scene, yet their role is almost insignificant. There is no communication between the two of you, and there is no real attempt to help each other to better experience life. Your relationships with such people are very informal and communication is almost nonexistent. However, the more you interact with them, the less informal your relationships become and the greater the importance of good communication skills.

You may also have a large network of acquaintances and friendships in your lifetime. These are the people with whom you form *personal* relationships. Although some people might have a pool of friends of upwards to 2,500 people, most of us have fewer than twenty friends whom we rely upon for close communication. For example, the average American married couple today has close friendships with about seven people. Thus, even though you may have some close friends you rely upon to discuss various matters, the number of very close friendships will be relatively small. Further, research shows that only a few of them will be effective communicators (Myrick and Sorenson, 1988).

Miss Manners believes that the secret of an unhappy marriage is communication.

Judith Martin

There is another group of people with whom you interact because you need to do so to accomplish some goal (e.g., to obtain a service provided by others). These interactions are conducted

---

within the context of *impersonal structured* relationships. When you go to a store to buy a pair of shoes, a relationship with the salesperson is involved, but it is a casual one. You may or may not strike up a conversation. If you do, more often than not your comments relate to the task of buying a pair of shoes. Although buying shoes is a personal matter and the salesperson is interested in helping you, communication between the two of you is usually safe and limited. It is not necessary to learn more about the other person's personality and special interests. Similarly, when you go to a doctor or dentist, you usually have a well-defined purpose. You are asking for certain professional services. After an examination, a few questions, and a diagnosis, the doctor provides a prescription or treatment. Again, the focus is usually upon a particular concern and you are relying entirely upon the professional judgment and expertise of the doctor. Good interpersonal communication with such a professional is always valuable, but it is not a prerequisite to obtaining the services sought. You trust these people to help you because they have either the credentials or the job position to offer service. In your interactions with them, there are accepted forms of communication and behavior. Both parties understand the limitations, the task, and the desire to speed things along (Myrick and Sorenson, 1988).

A good relationship has a pattern like a dance.... The partners do not need to hold on tightly, because they move confidently in the same pattern.... There is no place here for the possessive clutch, the clinging arm, the heavy hand; only the barest touch in passing.... Because they know they are partners moving to the same rhythm....

Ann Morrow Lindbergh

There is an increasing number of articles and books being written which describe how people in our society feel alienated from one another. Relationships of all kinds are encountering stress and strain, and becoming shorter in duration. It has been suggested that people are not sufficiently "involved" with others to satisfy their basic needs. More and more, people are leading fragmented lives and having trouble getting along with others. One striking solution to problems of isolation and alienation lies in better communication, particularly facilitative communication. However, facilitative communication is not always appropriate and needed for all types of relationships. Generally, facilitative communication is rarely used in *informal* relationships, and only in *impersonal structured* relationships when the circumstances invite it. However, facilitative communication can and should be used frequently to enhance *personal* relationships.

In summary, as human beings, we are social creatures. We interact with each other in many ways in order to satisfy our personal needs, and our interactions take various forms and patterns. Interpersonal communication pervades the very foundation of our existence as well as our potential growth as human beings.

It seems only logical that people should exchange thoughts and ideas and learn to understand one another better through communication. Yet many people have limited interpersonal skills and are not sure how to facilitate communication, especially when it involves people who appear to be very different from themselves. When we are defensive and resistant to learning, we build barriers between ourselves and others. Communication barriers distort ideas and create misunderstandings.

Facilitative communication results in greater understanding, acceptance, and appreciation. Therefore, it is absolutely essential for improving multicultural communication.

As we read, listen, observe, and open ourselves to experience, we establish the roots for a better understanding of ourselves and others. We learn to value uniqueness. One of the major reasons we experience problems in communication is that we sometimes neglect to remember that individual experiences are never identical. We will, ultimately, find more commonality than difference, regardless of our cultural differences, as we facilitate communication between us.

Individual Practice Activity

Who I Am:

The purpose of this exercise is for you to learn more about the members of your group or class and to help them to learn more about you.

Begin by printing your first name in the center of an index card. Write it large enough so other people can read it. In the upper left-hand corner, write or put a symbol for (a) where you were born and (b) a favorite place you would like to go. In the upper right-hand corner, put a symbol or write words which tell something you like to do to have fun. In the lower left-hand corner, write three words that your best friend might use to describe you. In the lower right-hand corner, describe one characteristic about your culture or race that you value and appreciate. Finally, put another symbol somewhere on your card which tells something you are looking forward to doing in the future.

Group Practice Activity

Instructor's Note:

Ask the participants to fasten (e.g., with a pin) the "Who I Am" card to the front of their shirts or blouses. Then, ask them to find an individual they do not know very well, preferably of different culture and gender, someone with whom they can pair up. These two "new found friends" should interview one another concerning the data on the cards for 4 or 5 minutes. Next, form a large circle with the pairs standing together. Each pair should in turn step forward and introduce one another to the group/class. You may want to ask the participants to wear their name tags to subsequent sessions until everyone knows everyone else.

Outside Assignments

1. Begin a diary concerning someone from a different cultural background than yours with whom you wish to begin or improve your interpersonal relationship. This individual should not be a member of this class/group. Make entries at least once a week. Your instructor may ask you to share the contents from time to time. It is best to use codes instead of personal names in your diary.

2. Read the poem "Stranger" by Peter Goblen (below) and answer the questions following it. Bring your responses to the next class/group meeting and be prepared to discuss your responses with others in your group.

Stranger

Stranger, do not come one step nearer
do not reach out toward me
stranger
we must not touch our hands
to join your loneliness and mine

Abide by the regulation:
    no man shall approach a man
    no woman shall approach a woman
    nor man, woman, nor woman, man
Our life depends on it

You wear a red scarf
I wear a blue cap
there can be nothing between us
If you ask me the time, I must turn my wrist
If I ask you the way, you must point

The rules hang from every lamppost
above the basket of geraniums
they are nailed into the telephone poles
Though we scream to break the silence
who would conjecture the universality of his sorrow
who would confess at the street corner

Stranger, at the time of fire
    you will pass through the smoke to save me
Stranger, at the time of flood
    I will lift you from the water
At the time of the invader
    we will gather together

Guard us from our intimacy
now, as we stand adjacent on the endless belt
conveying us into the future
which, like the ancients' heaven
will justify the disaster of this hour

Peter Goblen

1. What personal meaning does the poem have for you?

2. What was most striking about this poem?

3. What implications does the poem have for intercultural communication?

References

Stewart, J. (1986). *Bridges, not walls: A book about interpersonal communication,* 4th ed. New York: Random House.

Podesta, C. (1989). *Self-esteem and the six-second secret* (an audiotape). Manderville, LA: Communicare, Inc.

Myrick, R. and Sorenson, D. (1988). *Peer helping: A practical guide.* Minneapolis, MN: Educational Media Corporation.

Chapter *II*

Behavior and Communication

"Why do I do the things I do?" Have you ever asked yourself that question? It is a common question we often ask ourselves, especially when things are not going smoothly. No doubt there also have been times when you have observed others doing something that aroused your curiosity and you wondered: "What makes them do that?," "What makes them talk like that?," or "How can they act that way toward others?"

Human behavior is fascinating. We talk about it much of the time. But it is not only a popular topic of conversation, it also has been the subject of serious study. Psychologists and other scientists have been studying human communication behavior for a long time. However, more often than not their work has led to more questions than answers. We need to continue to study human communication and to search for ways to improve it.

This is not a chapter on "Everything You Wanted To Know About Human Communication Behavior But Were Afraid to Ask." Rather, I will cover only a few principles, concepts, and ideas which will help you to better understand how people learn, make decisions, change, develop their personalities, and communicate.

Understanding Human Behavior

Since this book is designed to help you to be a more effective communicator, and to understand and appreciate diversity and similarity, it is important to have a basis from which to work. Some human behavior concepts are generally universal across cultures and provide a foundation for building better communication skills and techniques.

While there may be other concepts which might be helpful, the following seven principles, selected from several studies and outlined and described by Myrick and Sorenson (1988), are relevant across most cultural groups, and provide understanding of people and their behavior:

1. **We all have basic needs.**
2. **Everything we do is goal-directed.**
3. **Our self-concepts influence our behavior.**
4. **Self-concepts are learned and can change.**
5. **Self-concepts are influenced by the consequences of what we do.**
6. **We are always learning and changing.**
7. **We learn from each other.**

Let us examine each of these principles in greater detail.

Principle 1: We all have basic needs

In order for us to have a sense of well-being and to experience success in life, several basic needs must be met. When these needs are unmet (i.e., not satisfied), we do not function well. When these needs are met, or satisfied, our productivity, personal development, interpersonal relationships, and general health are enhanced. The most obvious needs, of course, are those for food, water, elimination, sleep, and shelter. These are the human needs necessary for daily living for all humans, regardless of cultural background. The following needs also have been identified as essential, regardless of culture.

The need to be loved and accepted. Each of us wants to be accepted for who and what we are. We want our uniqueness to be appreciated by others; it is frustrating and disappointing when we are accepted only if we please others. We feel a beneficial warmth and strength when we experience unconditional love and acceptance. It is an experience that helps us say: "Hey, I'm okay and it feels great to be valued as a person."

Man lives by affirmation even more than he lives by bread.

Victor Hugo

The need for security. We learn and function best in situations where we feel safe and free from threat. It is not fun, for example, to be in a class where we are afraid that what we say might be ridiculed, or where we feel unaccepted because of our race or religion, or even where we feel secure only if our work is "mistake-proof." This latter fear is particularly influential for our behaviors. For fear of making a mistake, some people develop a shell around themselves in which very few are allowed to enter. Such a shell provides "protection" that gives a sense of comfort, even if it is limiting and prevents them from reaching out and enjoying new experiences. On the other hand, when people do not need a shell and feel secure from threat, there is a special joy in living.

Do your friends and others feel threatened by you? Are they afraid to expose who they actually are? Are they afraid that you will reject them? Unfortunately, we deny ourselves many opportunities and pleasures because of our fears of rejection. One of Charles Schultz's comic strips humorously illustrates this barrier to communication. The *Peanuts* children are lying on their backs on a hilltop looking at clouds and using their imagination. Linus states, assuredly, that he sees a map of British Honduras, the Taj Mahal and a profile of Thomas Eaking, the famous painter. Lucy indicates that she is impressed with Linus' imagination and asks Charlie Brown to tell the group what he sees. Charlie responds dejectedly, "Well, I was going to say I saw a ducky and a horsie, but I changed my mind."

The need to belong. As noted, each of us, regardless of culture, has the need to belong to some kind of group; being a part of a group gives us a sense of identity. It may be a particular sub-cultural group, school group, or church group. Group membership helps us feel accepted, and provides support needed to help reduce anxiety. For example, "self-help" groups, such as Alcoholics Anonymous, Gamblers Anonymous, Alateen, and so forth, abound in America. For another example, there are students who upon arriving at school immediately go to a favorite meeting place where they can meet with their friends. They find security and a sense of identity by talking with the group—*their* group. "Hey, what's happening?" is answered in a way that communicates understanding, shared interest, and *acceptance.* There also are formally organized groups, such as athletic teams, student union organizations, language clubs, music groups, Hispanic peer facilitators, sororities and fraternities, Black Student Unions, pep squads, and so forth that provide a source of identity and a sense of belongingness.

The need to take responsibility and to make choices. Another of our basic needs is to feel in control of our lives. The emotional experience of feeling in charge, of being able to be ourselves, is important. When this need is thwarted, we can become angry, devious, manipulative, self-sacrificing, and/or defensive. However, while the need to be independent and responsible is relevant across most cultural groups, it is recognized that some cultures place more emphasis on independence than others. Matter of fact, as you will read later in this book, some cultures place the welfare of the group over and above the needs of the individual. In those cultures, individual independence is not reinforced to the extent that it is in middle class America. However, it is believed that most "Americanized," assimilated cultural groups value individual responsibility highly.

Principle 2: Everything we do is goal-directed.

We all want to maintain and enhance our personal survival. Survival characterizes the essence of all living things. For example, a plant turns its leaves toward the sun and its root system toward water, particularly where there is limited water and sun available. Survival also plays a central role in learning and behavior.

What makes us human is the way we interact with other people. To the extent that our relationships reflect kindness, mercy, consideration, tenderness, love, concern, compassion, cooperation, responsiveness, and caring, we are becoming more human. In humanizing relationships, individuals are sympathetic and responsive to human needs. They invest each other with the character of humanity, and they treat and regard each other as human. It is positive involvement with other people that we label humane. In a dehumanizing relationship, people are divested of those qualities that are uniquely human and are turned into machines, in the sense that they are treated in impersonal ways that reflect unconcern with human values. To be inhumane is to be unmoved by the suffering of others, to be unkind, even cruel and brutal. In a deep sense, the way we relate to others and the nature of the relationships we build and maintain determine what kind of people we become.

David Johnson

We spend most of our lives trying to maximize our pleasure and minimize our pain. A seemingly simple idea, but apply it to your life. Is it not true that you tend to do those things most often that bring you some kind of pleasure or reward? We try to avoid punishment, whether it is physical or psychological. We protect our physical self and take precautions to avoid getting hurt. The same principle is true of psychological pain, which is almost always the result of a direct or indirect breakdown in communication with another human being.

It is important to remember that we not only change ourselves to help us survive physically, but we also change our behavior, the ways we make decisions, and the ways we communicate to increase "psychological-self" survival. The attitudes, ideas and perceptions we have about ourselves are organized, generally consistent, and are developed over a long period of time. The term self-concept is applied to this view of ourselves.

Principle 3: Self-concepts influence behavior.

Each of us has some kind of self-picture which plays a big role in how we communicate with others. This picture might best be described as "I" or "me." It is this self-concept, or self-image, that determines our behavior, including our communication patterns. No other person will ever come to know us the way we know ourselves. It is through our self-concepts that we perceive the world i.e., hold a worldview, regardless of cultural upbringing. That is, we feel, we think, and we act based upon our self-perceptions, which, most probably, are culturally determined.

Persons with Positive Self-Concepts:

1. Are likely to think well of others.
2. Expect to be accepted by others.
3. Evaluate their own performance more favorably.
4. Perform well when being watched; are not afraid of others' reactions.
5. Work harder for people who demand high standards of performance.
6. Are inclined to feel comfortable with others they view as superior in some way.
7. Are able to defend themselves against negative comments of others.

Persons With Negative Self-Concepts:

1. Are likely to disapprove of others.
2. Expect to be rejected by others.
3. Evaluate their own performance less favorably.
4. Perform poorly when being watched: are sensitive to possible negative reactions.
5. Work harder for undemanding, less critical people.
6. Feel threatened by people they view as superior in some way.
7. Have difficulty defending themselves against other's negative comments; are more easily influenced.

D. Hamachek

Your self-concept can be described in many ways: *I am*—your general nature; *I can*—your abilities; *I should or should not*—your beliefs and attitudes; or *I want to be*—your aspirations. You will behave and communicate in certain ways depending upon how you see yourself. When you act in a way not your usual custom, or perhaps contrary to the way you would like to be, then the experience is unpleasant, and you may begin to feel defensive, inadequate, insecure, and even worthless. Psychologists refer to this as "incongruence;" when your behavior does not really fit with "you."

Healthy persons are capable of deeper and stronger friendships, greater love and devotion than the average person. Although their friendships are more intense, they are fewer in number. Generally those with whom they associate are healthier and more mature than the average. Healthy persons find happiness in helping others and derive just as much satisfaction out of facilitating the growth and development of others as their own.

Melvin Witmer

Principle 4: Our self-concepts are learned and can change.

Self-concepts are learned and can change, although change is usually slow, often tedious, and painful. Once the self-concept becomes consistent, it is difficult to change because change brings threat, anxiety, and fear of self-destruction. However, people can and do change. We can change our feelings and behaviors toward those who are different from us. We can learn to value diversity and sameness. However, we have to "want" to change. Relatedly, as good communicators we can help others change, and in the process experience meaningful changes in our own lives.

Some parts of the self-concept can be attributed to heredity (e.g., physical size, color of skin, hair texture, or general physical features). Our self-concepts also are influenced by the culture and environment in which we live. Two children growing up in the same family might behave differently just as much as two children from different parts of the world because their *individually* unique environments and experiences influenced their *individual* self-belief systems. Each has a unique self-image, and behaves accordingly. However, with desire and appropriate training, we can communicate effectively, regardless of our individual or cultural differences.

Children Learn What They Live

If a child lives with criticism he learns to condemn.
If a child lives with hostility he learns to fight.
If a child lives with ridicule he learns to be shy.
If a child lives with shame he learns to feel guilt.
If a child lives with tolerance he learns to be patient.
If a child lives with encouragement he learns confidence.
If a child lives with praise he learns to appreciate.
If a child lives with fairness he learns justice.
If a child lives with security he learns to have faith.
If a child lives with approval he learns to like himself.
If a child lives with acceptance and friendship he learns to
find love in the world.

Dorothy Law Nolte

Principle 5: Self-concepts are influenced by the consequences of what we do.

Rewards and punishments play important roles in determining how consistently we behave and how we learn. We do things most frequently that enhance our self-image. For example, if "talking tough" and getting into fights is part of how a person sees him [her] self, that will be a frequent behavior. Or, if being a scholar and investigating scientific hypotheses is a part of the self-concept, the person will spend a lot of time engaging in research activities.

It is thus with most of us; we are what other people say we are.
We know ourselves chiefly by hearsay.

Eric Hoffer

Much of what we do is shaped by our past as well as our immediate experiences, but nothing influences the development of our self more than the consequences of our behavior. If the consequences of our behaviors are rewarding, those behaviors likely will occur again, and perhaps become a pattern or habit. On the other hand, if our behavior is ineffective, and plays no part in meeting our basic needs or enhancing our survival, it may be disregarded and not become a part of our personality.

Perception determines our reality and our behavior. An interesting finding in the study of human behavior is that a person's "reality" is influenced by the person's self-concept. What is reality? Suppose you were shown a five-minute film and then you and others in your group were asked to describe what you saw happen. You would soon realize that your perception, although similar to others in many respects, was slightly different. Such variance in perception, for example, has made it difficult for witnesses in a criminal case to describe accurately what took place. How we see things determines how we behave. The question is, what causes us to see things in a certain way? The writer's theory is a simple one—as we *feel*, so we *perceive*, so we *behave*; i.e., I *feel*, I *see*, I *act*. You will read more about this in later chapters.

Principle 6: We are always learning and changing.

Learning is not limited to the classroom or to one particular culture. Learning is constant in all our lives. When you are not reading this book, for example, you are still learning—by watching, listening, communicating with others, or interacting with your surroundings. Learning is more than gathering and memorizing facts. It is more than learning information in a formal educational setting. It is the very act of living and surviving.

Principle 7: We learn from each other.

Most of our learning comes through interacting with others. People provide us with most of our rewards or punishments. We form relationships that are important in our lives. People serve as models whose characteristics we incorporate or reject. Without other people, learning is limited and would be bland, narrow, and unimaginative.

Man wishes to be confirmed in his being by man, and wishes to have a presence in the being of the other.... Secretly and bashfully he watches for a Yes which allows him to be and which can come to him only from one human person to another.

Martin Buber

If we truly desire to come to a better understanding of others and to value diversity, we need to make special efforts. We must want to accept people as they are, regardless of skin color, religion, cultural background, or whatever. We must accept their attitudes and beliefs as part of them—even though we may not necessarily agree with those attitudes. It also means that if we are going to effectively communicate with others, we cannot do it by pushing our world onto them or by forcing them to agree with our perceptions and decisions. We must see and accept their world-views without evaluation or judgment. To communicate effectively we must understand and appreciate how others view and react to their worlds, as opposed to telling them how they *should* view and react to their worlds. Implementing this perspective takes skill, but with practice it becomes part of everyday responding to others.

The needed approach is communicating facilitatively, which places a premium on understanding, appreciating, and accepting others regardless of how different they may be from us. It emphasizes that change comes about best when others gain personal insight through their own experiences rather than through our beliefs of who they are, what they want out of life, and what they are willing to do to get it. Interestingly, these requirements are critical for facilitative communication, both with those who are like us and with those who are culturally different.

Individual Practice Activity

Complete the following scale by placing an "A" and a "D" on the appropriate line for each set of the two opposing descriptive characteristics. You should respond as honestly as possible so as to increase your self-awareness. Place an "A" (Actual) on the *SOLID* line indicating where *you actually are* as a communicator and a "D" (Desired) on the *DOTTED* line directly beneath it to indicate where *you would like to be* as a communicator. That is, respond to each set of opposing words twice, once as you actually are and once as how you would like to be. For example, for the first set of words, if you see yourself "a little more negative than the average person," you would place an "A" on the *SOLID* line somewhere around 5 or 6. However, if you desire to be "very positive" you would place a "D" on the *DOTTED* line somewhere around 1 or 2. Bring your completed profile to the next class/ group meeting and be prepared to share it with others.

Me as a Communicator

(Actual "A" and Desired "D")

1   2   3   4   5   6   7

positive _____ negative

positive --- negative

honest _____ dishonest

honest --- dishonest

introverted _____ extroverted

introverted --- extroverted

fluent _____ diffluent

fluent --- diffluent

friendly _____ unfriendly

friendly --- unfriendly

loud _____ quiet

loud --- quiet

open _____ closed

open -- closed

tense _____ relaxed

tense --- relaxed

intellectual _____ nonintellectual

intellectual ------------------------------------ nonintellectual

static _____ changeable

static --- changeable

calm _____ excitable

calm --- excitable

empathic ___ _____ unempathic

empathic -- unempathic

listener _____ non-listener

listener --- non-listener

Me as a Communicator (continued)

conservative _____ liberal

conservative --- liberal

hard _____ soft

hard --- soft

unbiased _____ biased

unbiased --- biased

humorous _____ serious

humorous --- serious

soft _____ loud

soft -- loud

prejudiced _____ non-prejudicial

prejudiced ------------------------------------- non-prejudicial

shallow _____ deep

shallow --- deep

strong _____ weak

strong --- weak

kind _____ unkind

kind -- unkind

accepting _____ nonaccepting

accepting --- nonaccepting

optimistic _____ pessimistic

optimistic --- pessimistic

ferocious _____ peaceful

ferocious --- peaceful

Group Practice Activity

Instructor's Note:

Divide the participants into small groups of 5 or 6 each. Each group should elect a leader to lead a group discussion on the above survey *"Me as a Communicator."* Set the following ground rules for each group:

1. Share your ideas, thoughts, and feelings.
2. Listen to each other's ideas, thoughts, and feelings without interruption, judgment, advice giving, interpretation, or evaluation.
3. Anyone can pass at any time (i.e., not respond or share).

Outside Assignment

There are many methods that can be used to assess or evaluate yourself, including taking a personality inventory, completing a values checklist, writing a personal essay, listing your strengths and weaknesses, or asking others how they see you.

Because your self-concept influences your communicative behavior, it is important to know more about it. Self-concepts are highly personal and we often find it difficult to verbalize ours to others. However, attempts at describing yourself to others can bring about insights about the things you do, how you communicate, and the decisions you make. It is important to remember that our self-concepts do change from time to time.

Following is a self-appraisal inventory. Find a private place and complete the inventory. Mark it as you see yourself now. Sometimes it is helpful to mark the first response that comes to mind. Be as candid and honest with yourself as you can. Being candid and honest is an important first step in understanding your self-concept. Bring your completed inventory to the next class/group session and be prepared to discuss your evaluation of self. This inventory was adapted from Myrick and Erney (1984).

Self-Appraisal Inventory

Instructions:

For each of the statements below, check the place on the scale which best describes your opinion (SA = Strongly Agree, A = Agree, NS = Not Sure, D = Disagree, SD = Strongly Disagree)

SA A NS D SD 1. I have the ability to listen to others.

SA A NS D SD 2. I feel comfortable sharing my feelings with others.

SA A NS D SD 3. I have some understanding of why I do the things I do.

SA A NS D SD 4. I am tolerant of others regardless of their culture or race.

SA A NS D SD 5. I am curious about what others think and feel.

SA A NS D SD 6. It is easy for me to be accepting of others' behaviors.

SA A NS D SD 7. I trust most people.

SA A NS D SD 8. I have an ability to influence others.

SA A NS D SD 9. I get along well with my peers.

SA A NS D SD 10. I have a clear idea of my goals in life.

SA A NS D SD 11. I know what I value and believe to be true.

SA A NS D SD 12. I work well alone and independent of others when I need to.

SA A NS D SD 13. I can accept criticism from others.

SA A NS D SD 14. I care about my appearance.

SA A NS D SD 15. I am curious about what others think of me.

SA A NS D SD 16. I am optimistic about my future.

SA A NS D SD 17. I am happy with my cultural group.

SA A NS D SD 18. I feel secure in my relationships with others of a different race.

SA A NS D SD 19. I am accepting of others regardless of their race, culture, or religion.

SA A NS D SD 20. I am open to all people.

Instructor's Note:

Divide the class into small groups of 5 or 6 and set the same guidelines for discussion as for previous activities.

Joe Wittmer, Ph.D.

Outside Assignment

This activity will help you to learn more about members of a race or culture different from your own. Suggested activities include, but are not limited to, the following:

1. Arrange to meet with a community leader with a cultural background different from yours and try to determine that person's perception of the needs and concerns of the group represented.

2. Talk with a college or high school student from a different culture regarding his or her needs and the most critical issues facing that person today.

3. Visit an ethnic community in your area and interview some of the people to find out about their concerns, needs, stresses, and outlook for the future.

4. Survey an ethnic group on how their group views *your* own cultural group.

What insights did you gain? What knowledge? What are your reactions? Come to the next class meeting with your *written* responses and be prepared to discuss them with others (adapted from Parker, 1988).

References

Hamachek, D. (1982). *Encounters with others.* New York: Holt, Rinehart and Winston.

Johnson, D. W. (1986). *Reaching out: Interpersonal effectiveness and self-actualization.* Englewood Cliffs, NJ: Prentice-Hall.

Myrick, R.D. and Erney, T. (1984). *Caring and sharing: Becoming a peer facilitator.* Minneapolis, MN: Educational Media Corporation.

Myrick, R.D. and Sorenson, D.L. (1988). *Peer helping: A practical guide.* Minneapolis, MN: Educational Media Corporation.

Parker, W.M. (1988). *Consciousness-raising: A primer for multicultural counseling.* Springfield, IL: Thomas.

Witmer, J. M. (1985). *Pathways to personal growth.* Muncie, IN: Accelerated Development.

Chapter *III*

Nonverbal Behaviors and Interpersonal Communication

Our language, socioeconomic class, race, ethnicity, and other cultural-related factors interact sometimes to create problems in interpersonal communication. One facet of communication, the impact of which is often neglected, is our nonverbal behavior. What we say and mean are enhanced, qualified, and/or illuminated by what we do (i.e., our nonverbal communication behaviors). Facial gestures, intonations, inflections, postural movements, and/or eye contact can strengthen or hinder the communication of personal messages. Nonverbal behaviors are complex and their meanings can vary across cultures. It would be erroneous to assume that nonverbal behaviors are universal and have the same meaning.

Each individual in a relationship is constantly commenting on his definition of the relationship implicitly or explicitly. Every message exchange (including silence) defines the relationship implicitly since it expresses the idea this is the sort of relationship where this sort of message may be given.

Donald Jackson

Body Language Hype

Almost every bookstore in America has self-help books on improving body language or how to better read the body language of others. Authors of such books make all sorts of promises to help you learn how to improve your social, sex, and business lives. "All you have to do is learn how to read another's body language," they proclaim.

You can see phrases for similar claims on magazine covers, such as, "What is Your Body Saying to Other People?", or "What Signals are You Giving to People?" Wanting to sell books or magazines, they claim that their "secrets" to body language will help you learn the personal secrets of others, from your best friends to total strangers! Obviously these authors believe nonverbal body language is important in interpersonal communications. That is certainly true, but not in the sense that they have proposed them.

The Impact of Nonverbal Messages

Research on nonverbal communication has demonstrated that in a normal two-person conversation, verbal components (i.e., words) convey only between 7 and 20 percent of the meaning of the message. The majority of communication meaning between two people is conveyed nonverbally, to the extent of being greater than 80% of the communication impact! Our dress, posture, silence, facial expressions, intonations, eye contact, hand and body movements, tone of voice, pauses, spatial distance, and touch all are important aspects in the ways in which we communicate. Therefore, if we are to be successful in facilitative communication, we must become fully aware of the ways in which we and others "talk" nonverbally. It is also important to become aware of differences in nonverbal communication across cultures.

Albert Mehrabian (1969) argued that the total impact of a communication, or message meaning actually communicated, is a function of the formula: **Total impact = 7% verbal + 38% vocal + 55% facial**. His formula involved very little influence attributed to words spoken. Approximately 93% of message impact is nonverbal!

Nonverbal Substitutes For Verbal Language

We often make nonverbal movements to communicate with another person instead of using words. For example, in the American culture we use nonverbal signs (i.e., motions) to indicate "disgust," "ok," "peace," "give directions," "hitch-hiking," "beckoning," "yes," "no," "uncertainty," or "go away!" And, we have some gestural communications that are classified as distasteful, e.g., sticking out our tongue, or vulgar in our American culture as a whole. Nonverbal behaviors often substitute for words or phrases. Even though we use them frequently, however, we may not be consciously aware of them. They are frequently learned through a process of conditioning. That is, nonverbal behaviors, and their associated messages, are usually learned unconsciously by imitating those around us.

Some nonverbal behaviors may be offensive to culturally distinct individuals. For example, while teaching in Columbia, South America, a few years back, during a lecture, I made reference to the size of one of my Colombian colleagues by extending my right arm out with the palm face down. My gesture was an attempt to indicate that the person was small in stature. However, the members of my college level class, all Colombian, gasped. In Columbia, the outstretched hand with the palm down is a nonverbal signal for indicating the size of animals, never used for indicating the size of people! In that part of the world, the size of people is indicated by extending the arm out with the palm vertical and the thumb pointing upward. For another example, consider the "A-OK" gesture which can be given by joining thumb and forefinger on the right hand to form a small circle. Most Americans view this as a happy affirmation. However, the same nonverbal sign has negative meanings in other parts of the world. In Greece, it is a vulgar sexual invitation and is considered insulting. In France and Belgium, such a display means "you are worth zero," or "your IQ is zero," both of which are intended to be insults (Adler, Rosenfeld & Towne, 1989).

Smiling is an expression which usually indicates liking or positive affect. However, laughing does not necessarily imply happiness. It may be meant to indicate other emotions such as embarrassment, discomfort, or shyness. And, as noted, some Asian American groups believe smiling implies weakness or temerity (Sue & Sue, 1990). Other nonverbal responses are also culturally determined, i.e., to reveal respect Anglos stand, while in Fiji sitting shows respect for one's elders. And, it is obvious that nonverbal signs for sexual attractiveness differ from culture to culture, i.e., size of breasts, fatness or thinness, and so forth.

Among the Japanese and Chinese, restraint or suppression of strong feelings, such as anger, irritation, sadness, love, or happiness, may be considered a sign of maturity and wisdom. Thus, oriental children are taught that outward emotional expressions, including associated facial expressions, body movements and verbal content, are inappropriate (Sue & Sue, 1990).

Some, perhaps most, of our nonverbal behaviors are used to accompany and illustrate certain verbal messages. For example, there is often a movement of the head or hands in a certain direction when we say "let's go." Or, we can indicate that we "don't want to go." In describing a circle we often make a circular motion with our hands. When we are not in a talking mood, or want someone to leave us alone, we often indicate our feelings nonverbally, i.e., not paying attention. When we want to say "yes" or "no" we often emphasize our intent with a movement of our head either vertically or horizontally. Or, we can say "maybe" or "not sure" with a shrug of our shoulders, tilt of our head, hand gestures, and so forth.

Frequently used nonverbal behaviors are conditioned in us by our culture, and it is very difficult to change them. Try saying "yes" while shaking your head from side to side or saying "no" while nodding your head up and down. However, we can learn how to better interpret, and, if appropriate, change nonverbal behaviors by paying careful attention to them in self and others. We all need to become more aware of our individual nonverbal behaviors and those of people of other cultures if we are to communicate effectively (Adler, Rosenfeld & Town, 1988).

Our Personal Space

Subtle differences in body language, such as behaviors interpreted differentially by culturally distinct groups, can damage our interpersonal relationships without us ever realizing what has gone wrong. For example, according to research, most American business persons tend to conduct business interactions at a distance of approximately four to five feet. Those from the Middle East, however, tend to stand much closer to the person with whom they are conversing. Imagine the Middle Eastern business person advancing to make a point in conversation while the American business person is retreating.... Can you see some potential problems that representatives from these two cultures would have? One would keep moving forward hoping to close the gap while the other would keep backing away! Both would feel awkward and uncomfortable, but not know why (Alder, Rosenfeld & Towne, 1989).

For many Hispanics, talking with another person involves a closer stance than many Anglos might find comfortable. Within an exchange under these circumstances, the Hispanic may view the Anglo as being cold and aloof, while the Anglo may interpret the Hispanic as being pushy. Similarly, while Anglos often shake hands when meeting, Latinos often use other forms of body contact (e.g., kissing, hugging) as a form of greeting in addition to the handshake.

Cultural groups vary greatly in how they use "personal space" in meeting and conversing. For example, Old Order Amish adult males exchange kisses to both cheeks when greeting one another, a process which obviously brings the persons involved very close together. In traditional Asian culture, subtlety in expression is a highly prized art. Direct or confrontive communication, particularly that bringing the persons talking very close together, is viewed as lacking in respect and sensitivity, and a crude form of communication. For many Latin Americans, Africans, Indonesians, Arabs, South Americans, and French, conversing with a person involves a closer stance than normally comfortable for Northwest Europeans (Sue & Sue, 1990). "Personal space," particularly that which is culturally distinct, is an important dynamic in effective, facilitative communication.

Eye Contact as Nonverbal Communication

Patterns of eye contact vary across cultures throughout the world and among various American culturally distinct groups. For example, in parts of Latin America it is appropriate to stare (i.e., maintain direct eye contact) at another person (referred to as "gazeholding") even if you are not engaging that person in conversation. Again, while teaching in Columbia, South America, I was made uneasy by "gazeholding" because it is not a common practice in the United States; it caused me to be embarrassed and confused about "what the message was." Anglo Americans, when meeting a stranger on the sidewalk, for example, have brief, indirect eye contact and then look away. However, on the sidewalks of Columbia, eye contact continues until one person is completely past the approaching person, even a stranger! When stopped at a traffic light in America we tend to glance at individuals in other cars stopped at the light and then quickly glance away. In Columbia eye contact is maintained until the light changes. This is the "norm," and to do otherwise may be considered rude. In direct opposition to the Colombian culture, many Asians, Indians, Pakistanis, and Northern Europeans gaze at the person to whom they are talking only peripherally, if at all. Being unaware of culturally diverse uses of eye contact may make both the listener and the talker uncomfortable, and adversely effect communication.

Anglo Americans rely heavily on eye contact as a part of communication. However, researchers have found that Black Americans assume being in close proximity to the other person is enough to indicate attentiveness. That is, to them, looking at the person directly is not necessary to indicate interest in what is being said. According to Sue and Sue (1990), white, middle class Americans avoid eye contact about 50% of the time when talking to others. However, when listening, they maintain eye contact more than 80% of the time. The opposite is true for most Black Americans who have greater eye contact when speaking and considerably less eye contact when listening. Thus, the tendency to maintain less eye contact when communicating should not be misconstrued as hostility, inattentiveness, or disinterest. Because nonverbal "cues" usually occur outside our conscious awareness, it is important to bring nonverbal cues into self-awareness prior to interpretation.

Different cultures have different meanings for the directness of a gaze. Traditional Navajo groups use peripheral vision (i.e., indirect eye contact), and avoid eye contact if possible, in conversing. Some Navajos consider direct stares as hostile, a technique used to chastise children. In addition, Navajo children avoid eye contact with their elders as it shows disrespect. Similarly, among Mexican Americans and the Japanese, avoidance of eye contact may be a sign of respect or deference. Unknowingly ascribing "negative" motives, such as inattentiveness, rudeness, aggressiveness, shyness, or low intelligence, to such behavior hinders effective interpersonal communication (Sue & Sue 1990).

Some Cross Cultural Universal Nonverbal Behaviors

Many nonverbal behaviors appear to be "cross-cultural" (i.e., interpreted similarly in different cultures) and have the same meaning around the world. For example, broad smiles and laughter are generally considered universal "signals" of positive emotions. Conversely, frowns usually convey displeasure. Darwin (1872), the renowned evolutionist, believed that these two emotional expressions were inherited. He felt they were "survival" mechanisms permitting humans to convey important emotional states to others before learning how to speak. However, it should be acknowledged that certain cultures do not always view smiling in a positive manner, i.e., Sue and Sue (1990), as noted previously, stated that in certain instances, Asian Americans see smiling as suggesting weakness.

Children born deaf and/or blind display a broad range of so-called "normal" expressions. When happy, they smile and laugh, and when unhappy, they cry just as fully able bodied infants do.

We do communicate with our bodies even when we are not aware of it. The way we walk or stand or sit, the way we arch our eyebrows, the way we cock our heads, the way we purse our lips, the way we gesture with our hands—all of these are signals which accompany our verbal messages. When these signals speak in opposition to what we are saying with our mouths—and they often do—people cannot believe what we are saying.

John Killinger

It should be noted that while I believe that many nonverbal expressions are universal, nonverbal displays of feelings and emotions vary greatly among cultures. Overt demonstrations of feelings are not permitted as readily in some cultures as in the white, middle class American culture. However, members of some culturally distinct groups reveal feelings even more overtly than do white, middle class Americans. For example, as noted, in the Old Order Amish culture, adult men exchange the "Holy Kiss" when meeting. However, in contrast, Amish couples would *never* publicly show any signs of endearment (Wittmer, 1990).

Similarly, we know that Italians tend to hug one another when meeting. These behaviors are often frowned upon, and even made fun of, by many Americans. We also should be aware that not showing one's emotions does not mean that feelings are not present. For example, a Japanese individual might appear more controlled and placid than an Arab when meeting a best friend. However, their feelings are most probably identical in such situations (Adler, Rosenfeld & Towne, 1989).

The Universal Need for Touch

It was recently revealed that premature infants who were massaged for 15 minutes three times a day gained weight 45% faster than infants left alone in their incubators. Obviously, touch is quite important to human beings, and may even be the most important of our senses. The importance of touch is reflected in touch metaphors, of which there are many. We hear people say, "It was touch and go," or "I was deeply touched (by another's behaviors)," and we even hear people talk of "losing touch!" Human touch behaviors are probably instinctive because they occur soon after birth; newborns touch frequently with lips and hands. Human touch seems to be as essential to each of us as food and water. We "stay in touch" through both verbal and nonverbal behaviors. Does it feel good when someone touches you on the shoulder and tells you things will be all right? Does the touch greatly enhance the verbal message? The answer is "yes" for members of some cultural groups, i.e., Hispanics, but may be "no" for members of other groups. In addition, how and where we touch is important in some cultures. For example, in some Moslem countries the right hand is considered the "clean" one; used for eating, while the left hand is the "unclean" one; used in aiding the process of elimination. Thus, to touch, or offer some-one a gift with the left hand, may be offensive and even insulting (Sue & Sue, 1990). These examples indicate very clearly our need to cognitively understand the values and ways of other cultures if we hope to communicate effectively with participants from those cultures.

Nonverbal Behaviors and Emotions

Nonverbal behavior is a primary way of expressing human emotions. Facial expressions, for example, often "give us away" when we are trying to present a false image or message. Through our facial (and other) muscles we readily show anger, fear, happiness, surprise, eagerness, fatigue, and literally all human emotions. Our body postures (e.g., forward body trunk lean), gestures, and use of personal space all are often reflections of our emotions.

Various verbal facilitative responses can sometimes be difficult to use because their use requires that we be empathic listeners, that we understand beyond the words what another person is saying. Appropriate and accurate interpretation of another person's nonverbal "cues" is one way of really "hearing" what the person is saying. Sometimes it is initially difficult to really understand a person's messages because the person says one thing but behaves in ways inconsistent with the words. For example, sometimes a friend may say to you "that would be great," but somehow you doubt your friend's sincerity. It may be that the tone of voice, lack of eye contact, expressionless face, or a host of other nonverbal cues are causing your doubt.

Fortunately, there are not a whole lot of nonverbal behaviors that play significant roles in interpersonal communication. Unfortunately, they are usually ambiguous, and the facilitative person must take care not to rely solely on them for an accurate understanding of message meanings. Some of our nonverbal behaviors have several, possibly even opposite meanings. For example, a blush may represent embarrassment, pleasure, or even anger and hostility. As noted, tears can be expressions of joy, hurt, sadness, or anger.

It is important in facilitative communication to work at being accurate in interpreting nonverbal behaviors because it is obvious that we can make nonverbal behaviors mean two or more very different things. For example, we can give an affectionate wink in a flirting mode or wink at someone to mean that we are putting them on, or even lying (Adler, Rosenfeld & Town, 1984). Thus, in attempting to understand someone's nonverbal communication, it is essential that full recognition be given to both the person's culture and the context in which the message was given.

Although making appropriate verbal responses is crucial for facilitative communication, many people have difficulty in clearly and accurately communicating (verbally) how they feel. This is not surprising because the American society does not readily encourage open expression of feelings. Have you ever heard someone say, "Oh, he's just too emotional" or "To keep yourself from being hurt, you've got to hide your feelings." Our society appears to value "rational" thoughts and decisions more than feelings. However, you may also have heard the statement, "She wears her feelings on her sleeve." For some, feelings are expressed easier in nonverbal than in verbal ways.

In comparing verbal and nonverbal language, the latter is really quite limited (excluding the hearing impaired) for responding to others. However, we do know that nonverbal messages often communicate feelings and preferences, and support or contradict verbal messages.

When Verbal and Nonverbal Messages are Incongruent

As stated, we cannot *not* communicate and we communicate both verbally and nonverbally. Sitting quietly in a corner and reading a book communicates to others just as surely as saying, "Look, I want to read so leave me alone!" Staring out the window during class gives the teacher a message, such as that you are bored, thinking about something else, or just not interested. Such nonverbal messages are difficult to read. The teacher is not really sure what is going on with you. However, if you were to extend your arm outward, thumb pointing down, with a continuous up and down motion, most American teachers would get the idea! We need to be very careful in interpreting nonverbal behaviors. They do not always mean what we think they mean.

As a psychologist I rely more on physical signs to know what a person is like than on what comes out of his mouth, for often a person is so much out of touch with himself that he is unable to express his true feelings verbally. The nonverbal level is less subject to self-deception than the verbal level.

Frederick Perls

Can you tell when someone genuinely cares for you? Often that person's nonverbal messages tell you earlier, and more, than do verbal messages. In interpersonal communication, small movements, such those by eyes, hands, and facial muscles, "say" just as much, if not more, than do gross movements of gesturing, sitting in a corner, staring out a window, or jumping up and down. These small nonverbal movements are extremely important in interpersonal relationship communications. Thus, we need to be particularly careful that our nonverbal and verbal messages communicate and mean the same things. When communication "breaks down," it is often because our verbal and nonverbal messages are not congruent with one another. For example, if you are telling someone that you like that person while your eyes are down cast, your message of liking probably will not be accepted. Your actions are speaking louder than your words!

We Trust Nonverbal Behaviors More Than Verbal Behaviors

Generally, research has shown that when the verbal and nonverbal messages differ, or are incongruent, we are more apt to believe the nonverbal message. Have you ever watched a friend—say his name is Tom—in a conversation with a teacher, perhaps in a concealed attempt to get a low grade changed to a higher grade? Perhaps Tom really did not like the course very much, goofed off too much, but began the conversation by telling the teacher how hard he had worked, how much he liked the teacher, the class, and so forth. It is likely that as you observe Tom, he will give away his "real intentions" with various eye and facial movements and/or lack of eye contact. Most likely the teacher noticed too, and was left with a feeling that Tom's nonverbal behavior was much more believable than his verbal behavior!

Sue and Sue (1990) indicated that, as a group, African-Americans tend to accept that nonverbal communication is a more accurate barometer of true feelings and beliefs than verbal behavior. Sue and Sue also observed that Black Americans therefore are better able to read nonverbal messages than Anglo Americans, and to rely less on intellectual verbalizations to "make a point" in interpersonal communications. Anglos, on the other hand, tune in more to verbal than nonverbal messages. Because of lessened reliance on nonverbal messages and cues, greater verbalizations are needed to get a point across. If we are ignorant and insensitive to these differences, we are prone to feel that African Americans are unable to communicate except in simple terms.

Silence

For many Anglo Americans, silence is uncomfortable and/or embarrassing. Although Anglo Americans may say tritely that "silence is golden," they work hard at filling every moment with talk! Other cultures value silence much differently. Did you know that silence represents agreement among parties in France and

Russia, and as a method to observe privacy among Arabs? Silence is a sign of respect for elders in Asian cultures. In Japan, silence infers that the talker desires to continue talking after making a point (Adler, Rosenfeld & Town, 1989). To be effective communicators with those culturally different from us, it is important to know how silence is used by them.

Writer (to movie producer Sam Goldwyn): Mr. Goldwyn, I'm telling you a sensational story. I'm only asking for your opinion, and you fall asleep. Goldwyn: Isn't sleeping an opinion?

In this chapter I wrote about the importance of your skill to "read," "understand," and "be aware" of another's nonverbal behaviors. However, this is only one important component for facilitative communication. It is also important to be aware of our own nonverbal messages and behaviors, and to work to send accurate nonverbal cues to others as well. In addition, it is important to be aware of how culture influences nonverbal behavior. In facilitative communication, we must try to keep verbal and nonverbal messages congruent, and work to convey both messages accurately.

Outside Activity

How Do You Express Your Feelings?

Listed below are "feeling" words. In Column A, list a **synonym** for the feeling word in the first column. In Column B list at least two ways (i.e., behaviors) that you could use to convey that feeling nonverbally. Be prepared to share your responses with others in the class/group.

Feeling	Column A	Column B
Unhappy		
Tense		
Loving		
Excited		
Kind		
Lonely		
Frustrated		
Interested		
Angry		
Confident		
Calm		
Accepting		
Anxious		
Defensive		
Prejudicial		
Confused		
Warm		
Biased		
Tired		
Playfulness		
Submissive		
Irritated		
Rejecting		
Arrogance		
Timid		

Group Practice Activity

Instructor's Note:

Divide the participants into groups of 5 or 6 and request that they share their responses to the activity presented above. Remind them to "tune into one another's feelings, thoughts and ideas," and that anyone may pass a turn.

Outside Activity

Asian and Western Values

Look carefully at the two opposing lists below and answer the questions that follow. Bring your *written* responses to the next session and be prepared to share them with others.

Asian	Western
We live in time.	You live in space.
We are always at rest.	You are always on the move.
We are passive.	You are aggressive.
We like to contemplate.	You like to act.
We accept the world as it is.	You try to change it according to your blue print.
We live in peace with nature.	You try to impose your will on her.
Religion is our first love.	Technology is your passion.
We delight to think about the meaning of life.	You delight in physics.
We believe in freedom of silence.	You believe in freedom of speech.
We lapse into meditation.	You strive for articulation.
We marry first, then love.	You love first, then marry.
Our marriage is the beginning of a love affair.	Your marriage is the happy end of a romance.
It is an indissoluble bond.	It is a contract.

Our love is mute.	Your love is vocal.
We try to conceal it from the world.	You delight in showing it to others.
Self denial is a secret to our survival.	Self assertiveness is the key to your success.
We are taught from the cradle to want less and less.	You are urged every day to want more and more.
We glorify austerity and renunciation.	You emphasize gracious living and enjoyment.
Poverty is a badge of spiritual elevation.	It is to you a sign of degradation.
In the sunset years of life we renounce the world and prepare for the hereafter.	You retire to enjoy the fruits of your labor.

(FACD Guidelines, July, 1991)

1. Summarize, in one paragraph, the difference in values between the Asian and Western cultures as given above.

2. How might these differences impede communication between an Asian American and an Anglo American.

3. Select the nonverbal opposites found in the two lists above and indicate how they might affect your communication with an Asian American.

Group Practice Activity

Individual participants should find someone in the group/ class about whom they know very little, preferably someone of another sex and culture. Then the pairs should respond to the following questions about each other *without talking - i.e., in complete silence.*

What is your new friend's favorite:

1. TV program?
2. subject in school?
3. food?
4. type of car?

Does your new friend:

1. Handle money well?
2. Have a significant other? Is your friend married?
3. Have children? Plan to have children?_____

Now, get together with your new friend and verbally compare your responses—talk about them.

References

Adler, R., Rosenfeld, L., and Towne, N. (1989). *Interplay: The process of interpersonal communication.* New York: Holt, Rinehart, and Winston, Inc.

Darwin, C. (1872). *The expression of emotions in man and animals.* London: John Murray.

Mehrabian, A. (1972). *Nonverbal communication.* Chicago, IL: Aldine-- Atherton.

Wittmer, J. (1990). *The gentle people: personal perceptions on Amish life.* Minneapolis, MN: Educational Media Corporation.

Sue, D.W., and Sue, D. (1990). *Counseling the culturally different: Theory and practice.* New York: John Wiley.

The challenge of multicultural counseling. (July, 1991), *FACD Guidelines.*

Chapter *IV*

Multicultural Communication

Feelings, thoughts, nonverbal behaviors, and ideas are important in interpersonal communication and are culturally influenced and learned. Empathy, interest in others, caring, personal awareness, and understanding are stressed as important to effective interpersonal communication throughout this book. However, having these core conditions present is not always enough for effective communication with a person from another race or culture. We also need *cognitive empathy*. That is, knowledge of that person's culture, or knowing "where that person is coming from" is also extremely important. Later in this book you will learn about the characteristics of some cultural groups found in America today in greater detail. However, I wish to emphasize that cultures are made up of individual members. Thus, regardless of yours or the other person's cultural background, it is important to remember that the person with whom you are communicating is first of all another human being with many of the same needs, wants, and desires that you have!

People fail to get along because they fear each other. They fear each other because they don't know each other. They don't know each other because they have not properly communicated with each other.

Martin Luther King, Jr.

How important is it for us to be knowledgeable concerning different cultures? Did you know that by the year 2000 the Hispanic population in America will increase 21%, the Asian population 22%, the African American population 12% and the White population only 2%? Did you know there are 27,000,000 African Americans today and that this nation's largest school districts are made up of predominantly Black and Hispanic students? Were you aware that by the year 2000 one in three Americans will be non-white? By the year 2010 Hispanics will become the largest ethnic group in America and that by the year 2060 white Anglo Americans will be in the minority. You may think Jones is a common surname. Did you know that in the San Jose, California, the Vietnamese surname NGUYEN outnumbers JONES in the 1991 telephone directory, 14 columns to eight?

These figures indicate that many cultural groups are increasing in number rapidly in our country. However, many are still misunderstood. Why is lack of understanding of different cultures still found in the United States today? Much of the misunderstanding may stem from societal standards that were set by those who believed that everyone either is like them, or should be. That is, we sometimes assume they are or should be like us! However, if we have good knowledge of cultural backgrounds, we will understand better the sources and reasons for different peoples' behaviors—even those which appear odd or peculiar to us at times. This knowledge base, along with learning the facilitative communication skills given later in this book, will help us to understand better everyone's behaviors.

If everybody you invite into your life for a drink or dinner all look just like you, why not invite a friend from a different race or ethnic group to come to your house? If we could expand the horizon of people we respect, it would take us a long way toward ending racism. You cannot dislike, distrust or hate people you respect.

Former U.S. Representative
Barbara Jordan

Most culturally different group members do not want to be "mainstreamed," i.e., to develop white Anglo American middle-class values. Rather, they want to maintain their own identity and dignity. They want their difficulties and differences

---

Joe Wittmer, Ph.D.

to be understood rather than evaluated and changed. Their desire to be appreciated for who they are is just as strong as our desire to be appreciated for who we are.

Most personal experiences and perceptions are relevant only to the group in which one is reared, i.e., our personal cultural reference groups. This is probably why what is considered peculiar behavior in one cultural setting may be viewed as proper and necessary in another. Most of us are "culturally bound"—an idea we need to keep in mind as we learn more effective communication techniques for use with those who are culturally or racially different from us (Vacc, Wittmer, & Devaney, 1988).

Historical Influences and the Culturally Different

Culturally different groups frequently have been "politicized" and influenced by the social mood of the times. The dominant thought until the 1960s was that America was a "melting pot" of cultures. This is now recognized as the "melting pot myth." In actuality our own country is more like a "salad bowl" than a melting pot. Our social institutions, schools, and industries reflect the democratic ideal of providing opportunity for upward mobility for all who are deserving. An assumption underlying this thought during the 1960s was that cultural assimilation was "success" and cultural disassimilation was "failure." Unfortunately, assimilation connoted the unacceptability of minority populations' culture, language, and folkways in the United States. Today, a new interpretation relative to special populations is viewed with increasing favor. The democratic ideal, if imposed by the majority on individuals through education, serves to eliminate much that is good in society simply because it is different (Vacc, Wittmer, & Devaney, 1988). It will be difficult to change this perspective simply because Americans have a difficult time accepting "multi-cultures" existing in our country. That is, we tend to be more accepting of assimilated racial differences than we are of people of different cultures who want to retain their uniqueness, and therefore remain different.

The discernible interest of American's culturally different for recognition and preservation of their uniqueness, for whatever reasons, adds to the need for greater understanding of them. This understanding comes about best through communicating effectively with one another (Vacc, Wittmer, & Devaney, 1988).

America has a long history of oppression of minority groups. A case in point is Native Americans. The process of forced "assimilation" was actually funded by Congress in the early 1800s to promote "civilization among the aborigines." Not until the 1930s did the U.S. government's Bureau of Indian Affairs relax its efforts for "Americanization," and then it was only for a brief time (Vacc, Wittmer, & Devaney, 1988).

We have a history of treasuring our sameness, but we should also respect our diversity. Our histories should allow all students and teachers to feel like first-class citizens. A U.S. history that only stresses a westward movement across the continent would marginalize or exclude Native Americans. It would make African Americans ask, "Who booked my passage?" It would make Hispanics say, "We stood still and the border moved to the other side of us." And it would make Asian Americans wonder, "What about eastward movement rather than westward movement?"

Renato Rosaldo

Assimilation as an ideal under the "melting pot" philosophy has been basic to the American social system for many years, but particularly during and after World War I. During that period, many immigrants' children were made to feel ashamed of their family's speech, customs, and cultural values. Later, during the World War II era, heightened patriotism and fear of subversion caused the relocation and internment of hundreds of thousands of Japanese Americans (Vacc, Wittmer, & Devaney, 1988).

It was not until after World War II that the American society moved toward accepting individual differences. The landmark 1954 Supreme Court case of *Oliver Brown Vs. Board of Education* helped to begin the end of segregated schools. Starting with the Kennedy years in the 1960s, and more specifically during President Johnson's term of office, public policies and political forces gave impetus to the movement for individual rights. The *Economic Opportunity Act* and the *Civil Rights Act of 1964*, as well as the *Elementary and Secondary Education Act of 1965*, also helped foster rights for minority persons. No one act of legislation granted all "rights," but each contributed to a ripple effect for culturally different populations (Vacc, Wittmer, & Devaney, 1988).

Historical influences relative to the culturally different can easily be oversimplified and explained by simplistic slogans or by historians. This is not the intent of this book. To do so is to mock what is explicitly being sought by these groups; individuality and recognition of uniqueness.

Until late in the nineteenth century, this nation was considered by its majority to be a white Protestant country; at some time near the turn of the century, it became a white Christian country; after World War II, it was a white man's country. During the past several years it has become a multiethnic, multiracial country intensely aware of differences of every kind....

D. Ravitch

The emerging sense of worth of members of culturally distinct populations can no longer be neglected. Learning about their different values, attitudes, desires, aspirations, and beliefs is necessary because it effects all of us. Learning to communicate effectively with people from different cultures will speed up this necessary learning process.

Herein lies the tragedy of the age not that men are poor
All men know something of poverty
Not that men are wicked
Who is good?
Not that men are ignorant
What is truth?
Nay, but that men know so little

W.E.B. Dubois

Cultures: Alike but Different

Although members of different cultural groups are unique, different, and individual, there are similarities among culturally different persons. That is, beneath superficial characteristics, we usually find that there are more similarities than there are differences. Some experts suggest this is because all humanoids originated from a single species. It is probably true that there are more individual differences within racial groups than there are between groups. However, because various individual cultural groups do have different values, mores, interests, and world-views, we must acknowledge and understand them if we are to communicate effectively across cultural lines.

Individuals, regardless of their genetic makeup, ethnic heritage, or geographical location on earth, are in the same predicament. They confront the same basic survival problems. Housed in a frail, soft, naked body, humans exist in arid, frozen, rocky, fertile and tropical environments cluttered with a multiplicity of potentially destructive forces.

C. Vontress

Terms and Titles

Terms that have been widely used in the past to describe different cultural groups seem outdated and even oppressive, i.e., culturally deprived, culturally disadvantaged, and even "minorities." The term "culturally disadvantaged" seems to indicate that the person is somehow at a "disadvantage," and even lacks the cultural background necessary to ever become "advantaged." The term "deprived" suggests an absence of culture, and "minority" denotes "less than." Therefore, the terms "culturally distinct" and "culturally different" are preferred. Even these terms may carry negative connotations if used to imply that a person's culture is somehow out of step with the "majority" culture.

Joe Wittmer, Ph.D.

Some Cross-Cultural Communication Barriers

There are many barriers to communication between members of different cultures. However, one of the biggest problems is our own cultural encapsulation, i.e., the tendency to see things only one way, "our way," and to have difficulty in viewing events or ideas from other persons' frames of reference without bias.

The three barriers most often discussed in the communication literature are (a) language differences, (b) class-bound values, and (c) cultural-bound values. Language differences among the different cultural groups described in this book are many and varied. Communication is difficult unless we are sensitive to such differences. For example, reliance upon use of "standard English" with a bilingual individual may result in misperceptions of that person's strengths and weaknesses.

Differences in our values and those of a culturally distinct person may sometimes be due to a difference in "social" class. It is a well-known fact that many culturally different groups have been, and some still are, oppressed socially and economically in America. Class-bound values present unique problems in intercultural communication.

We frequently (though often unconsciously) impose our cultural values on people of different cultures and races, thus reflecting our insensitivity to their values. For example, we may believe that self-disclosure is an important condition for effective interpersonal communication, especially a relationship of long duration. On the other hand, culture may play a role in whether a person self-discloses readily to others. Self-disclosure may be contrary to the basic values of a cultural group. For example, Asian-American children are often taught at an early age to restrain from too much emotional expression. Thus, our request that they self-disclose their feelings to us may be threatening. The same interpersonal behavior training has been reported for Mexican-American individuals. Thus, even though the general American culture may be highly "verbal," and value emotional expression, not all people believe the same way.

Stereotyping and Communication

One of "mainstream" America's problems concerning different cultures is the tendency to stereotype. Stereotyping is a major
barrier to effective intercultural communication. When we stereotype someone we hold a rigid and fixed impression of a group
of people, which we then apply to all members of that group. The
many variations within the group are not considered.

In holding stereotypes, we become rigid and inflexible to
change. Stereotypes distort our ability to perceive other people
accurately. Thus, if we have been told and continue to believe
that, for example, all African Americans play loud music and
have lots of rhythm; or that all Native Americans drink too much;
or that Asian Americans are sneaky but make good scientists; or
that Anglos are cool, aloof, and can't be trusted; or that Hispanic
Americans are never on time; or that Jews are stingy, intelligent,
and loud; we will have difficulty communicating effectively with
individuals from those groups. In effect, if we believe these
stereotypes, then we will behave toward all members of such
groups as if they actually possess these traits. Even more unfortunately, some experts have said that one of the biggest problems
with stereotyping is that many members of culturally distinct
groups eventually come to believe the stereotypes about themselves, causing a negative, inferior sense of self-esteem.

It is never too late to give up your prejudices.

Henry David Thoreau

Self-Awareness and Communication with the Culturally Different

Our awareness and willingness to understand others is a major key to effective communication with culturally different people. We need to be aware of others' thoughts and feelings, regardless of their race, creed or cultural background. Effective, facilitative communicators are aware of other persons' frames of reference, their views of the world.

You can learn skills that will assist you in understanding how others view their worlds and react to them, as opposed to telling them how they *should* react and *behave* toward their own worlds! Their worldviews may be very different from yours, but they are based on their perceptions—which are their "realities." And, their reality determines how they feel, think and behave.

The *quality* of the relationship between you and a culturally different person may be the most important ingredient for effective communication. Relationships are enhanced if we are aware of the feelings we have towards those different from us. In addition, if we want to be effective communicators with such individuals, we need to work hard at changing any negative attitudes we may have about a particular culture of race. We need to look outside ourselves, step back, and take a hard look at ourselves! What do you see when you look in the mirror? A person who is open or biased? Someone who believes that those who are culturally different need to be "taken care" of?

It is very silly to teach someone the knowledge of the stars and the movement of the eighth sphere before teaching them the knowledge of themselves and their movements.

Montaigne

If you are an Anglo American, be aware that you may be viewed as a representative of a general society which has oppressed many culturally different groups. Culturally distinct individuals will know if you are condescending, untrustworthy, disrespectful, and/or if you have inappropriately low expectations for them. Any of these attitudes on your part will be recognizable and will be a barrier to communication.

Self-aware individuals avoid a condescending attitude and do not patronize culturally different persons. To patronize implies the belief that *we* hold a superior position to them—we come across to them as being "better" than they. And members of other cultural groups view this as disrespectful. Relatedly, some Anglo Americans seem to have a characteristic that could best be described as "assumed similarity." That is, they assume that people either ought to be like them or want to be like them! For example, I was born and reared for seventeen years as Old Order Amish. The Amish travel in horse drawn carriages, do not have electricity, and shun other such modern conveniences. I often give lectures to others concerning the Amish, and I am invariably questioned; "Are you telling us that members of your family *really* don't want television, telephones, cars, and so forth?" Believe me, they *really* do not. Be aware of your own "assumed similarity."

Psychologists indicate that we tend to give up our assumptions only after we have been confronted by data that shows our assumptions are wrong. We tend to search for evidence to support biased assumptions. Unfortunately, the reverse is seldom true. We do not often look for things to disprove erroneous assumptions. Self awareness is the key to changing the invalid assumptions we hold about other groups.

Cultural groups can be viewed objectively or subjectively. Certain cultures or groups have definite characteristics that can be seen. For example, married, Old Order Amish American males grow beards and, as noted above, sect participants travel by horse and buggy. These are objective and observable traits of that particular culturally distinct group. The subjective part of a culture is those beliefs, values, and opinions held by members of that culture. For example, the Amish have a deep sense of faith in their God. Faith is subjective and not readily observable. However, aware individuals realize that effective communication can help uncover and understand subjective traits, thus improving communication with members of particular cultural groups.

When I am aware that I experience feelings, thoughts, and behaviors, my self-understanding increases. When I become aware that you experience feelings, thoughts, and behaviors my understanding of you increases. And when I learn that you and I are both alike in this way, yet both individuals, my respect for us both increases.

Anonymous

Joe Wittmer, Ph.D.

There are many skills needed to be an effective multi-racial, multi-ethnic communicator. Communicating with those different from us must entail more than techniques or philosophy. We, as individual human beings, are the major ingredient. Our own philosophy of life, and self-awareness combined with skills and knowledge of the culture, yield the most effective communication.

Some Basic Guidelines and Assumptions

Vacc, Wittmer, and Devaney (1988) postulated the following guidelines which are basic to communicating effectively with individuals from culturally different groups:

1. Individual rather than mass methods and techniques of communicating with individuals are important regardless of the cultural group.

2. The individual, not the cultural group, is the unit of consideration. The individual is a person primarily, and an African American, for example, secondarily.

We are rapidly becoming a multi-ethnic society. And, all Americans must learn to communicate more effectively with one another, regardless of cultural or racial backgrounds. It is obvious that there are many communication barriers and these need to be addressed if our country is to survive. To move forward, we must respect one another's uniqueness, our sameness, and our differences; we cannot insist on being a "melting pot" society. The writer believes that among other things, accurate *information* and *knowledge* are essential and necessary as a foundation for communicating effectively with culturally distinct persons. The next four chapters contain such information and knowledge important to intercultural communication with participants from specific, diverse populations.

Outside Activity

Respond to the following questions in writing and bring your responses to the next class meeting.

1. When you hear the term *culturally different,* what group comes to mind first. Describe the participants of this culture in regard to their physical features, language, behaviors, attitudes, and lifestyles.

2. Think of the significant people in your life when you were a child (e.g., relatives, friends, or teachers). What do you remember about their attitudes toward other ethnic minority groups, i.e, African, Hispanic, Native, and/or Asian Americans? What can you hear them saying to you? What did you overhear that was intended for someone else's ears? What did you learn about these four groups from your (1) *parents?* From the (2) *movies?* What messages do (3) **you** give to others today about these *groups?*

3. Think of the cultural group to which you belong. When did you first become aware, and how did you learn that you were a member of a group that was different from other groups?

In Class Activity

Instructor's Note:

Divide the class members into small groups of 5 or 6 for the purpose of discussing the responses to the three questions posed above. Appoint a group leader and ask that person to lead the discussion based on the following points:

1. What have you learned, or relearned, about yourself by responding to the questions regarding different groups?

2. What are you aware of now about yourself or the groups?

3. What struck you most about this activity?

4. What did you learn about yourself that surprised you?

5. What did you learn about yourself that has the strongest implications for multicultural communication?

6. What experiences or events did you recall that have had the greatest impact on your present attitudes and feelings toward culturally distinct persons?

7. Now that you have brought many of these feelings to your awareness, what, if anything, would you like to change and/ or do (Parker, 1988)?

In Class Activity

Instructor's Note:

Divide the class into groups of ten and ask them to read the following and come to a *group* decision. Facilitate a discussion concerning their respective decisions.

The Shelter (Adapted from David Johnson)

Your group is in charge of experimental stations in the far outposts of civilization. You work in an important government agency in Washington, D.C. Suddenly volcanic eruptions occur all around the world; the world is being systematically destroyed as the sun is blotted out. People are getting into the available shelters. Your group receives a desperate call from one of your experimental stations. They ask for your help. There are eleven people at this station. But their "safe" shelter only holds six. They cannot decide which six people should enter the shelter. They have agreed that they will obey your group's decision as to which six people will go into the shelter and be saved. Your group has only superficial information about the eleven people and has *twenty* minutes to make the decision. You realize that the six people chosen *may be the only six left to start the human species over again.* Your group's decision, therefore, is vital to the continuation of our species. If your group does not make the decision within the twenty minutes allowed, all eleven people will die. Here is what you know about the eleven people:

1. Bookkeeper, white male, thirty-one years old
2. His wife, six months pregnant (race unknown)
3. Second-year medical student, male, militant Black American
4. Hollywood actress who is a singer and dancer (Black)
5. Biochemist, Native American female
6. Rabbi, fifty four years old, male
7. Olympic athlete, all sports, male (race unknown)
8. College student, white female
9. Policeman with gun (they cannot be separated) Race unknown.
10. College professor, male Hispanic (bilingual - Spanish and English)
11. Famous historian-author, forty-two years old, Asian male

Outside Assignment

Advanced Plan for Cultural Interaction

At the conclusion of the last chapter you were asked to develop a plan for becoming minimally involved with persons from a culturally or racially different group. However, this higher level plan will place you at a closer level of contact with culturally different individuals. This level presents a greater challenge, and requires you to establish a personal relationship with a culturally distinct individual.

The knowledge and skills gained through the previous action plan prepared you to interact with this person(s) more comfortably, avoiding many of the cultural blunders often made. The learning that occurs through the level two action plan is usually more intense than learning through superficial means.

A higher level action plan provides opportunity for you to have a cross-cultural experience at a more personal level. Through such activities many individuals have been able to confront and explore their own blocks, hang-ups, doubts, fears, and anxieties. Others have been able to gain more accurate knowledge and understanding by feeling free to raise and explore personal questions, issues, and concerns.

Some suggested action plans for the higher level might include:

1. Arrange to spend a week-end in the home of a culturally different family of your choice. Observe their family practices, values, interests, religious beliefs, disciplinary procedures, roles of family members, needs, issues, and concerns.

2. Set a meeting with a culturally different person with whom you have established rapport. Consider this meeting an opportunity to encounter many of your feelings, attitudes, and beliefs about this particular cultural group.

3. Plan and execute a major project with a culturally different person. The project should be mutually agreeable to both parties, and its goal should be to improve relations between the two groups (adapted from Parker, 1988).

Bring your written plan to the next session and be prepared to share it with a small group of peers.

Instructor's Note:

As with past activities, divide the participants into groups of 5 or 6 and set the following guidelines:

1. Tune into each other by listening closely.
2. Share ideas and feelings.

References

Johnson, D. W. (1986). *Reaching out: Interpersonal effectiveness and self-actualization.* Englewood Cliffs, NJ: Prentice-Hall.

Parker, W. M. (1988). *Consciousness-raising: A primer for multicultural counseling.* Springfield, IL: Thomas.

Section II

Cognitive Understanding of the Culturally Different: Views from the Inside

Chapter V

African Americans: Communication Styles and their Affect on Intercultural Communication

Eugia M. Littlejohn, M.Ed. Ed.S. and
Saundra B. Henderson, M.Ed. Ed.S.

Chapter VI

Cultural Perspectives in Communicating with Asian/Pacific Islanders

Mary A. Fukuyama, Ph.D. and
Chikako Inoue-Cox, Ph.D.

Chapter VII

Hispanic Americans

Cultural Perspectives in Communicating with Cuban Americans, Puerto Ricans, and Various Other Hispanic Americans

*Carlos A. Hernandez, M.Ed. Ed.S.
and Diane Estrada, M.Ed. Ed.S*

A Brief History, Current Problems, and Recommendations for Improving Communication with Mexican Americans

Antonio Avila, Ph.D.

Chapter VIII

Cultural and Historical Perspectives in Communicating with Native Americans

Patricia Stroud-Reifel, M.Ed.

Joe Wittmer, Ph.D.

In this section you will read about, and gain knowledge of, African Americans, Asian/Pacific Islanders, various Hispanic American groups, and Native Americans. These culturally distinct American sub-groups were selected because they are increasing in numbers more rapidly than any other special populations.

By the year 2050, the average US citizen will be of African, Hispanic, Asian, Pacific Island or Native American descent.

Barbara Van Blake

It has become trite to say that we live in a multi-racial, multi-cultural society, but, as the above quote indicates, it is the truth for the years ahead. By the year 2056, the "average" US citizen will trace his or her decent to Africa, Asia, the Hispanic countries, the Pacific Islands—almost anywhere but white Europe (Time Magazine, April 9, 1990).

The Hispanic population in the United States includes Mexican Americans, Puerto Ricans, and Cuban Americans; recent immigrants from El Salvador, Nicaragua, and the Dominican Republic; and immigrants from other Central and South American countries. The American public tends to regard Spanish-speaking people in the United States as one group because of their common language. However, as you will understand after reading Chapter Seven, people from each of these countries are quite different and do not regard themselves as a homogeneous group.

Hispanic groups constitute the second largest minority in the United States, after African Americans, the largest. Hispanics now represent eight percent of the total US population and are expected to become the largest minority group early in the next century (Prevention Review, 1991). And, Native Americans and Asian Americans are also increasing in number at a rapid pace.

Authors of the following chapters are writing from a particular perspective and are members of the respective subgroups of which they write. However, you are cautioned *not to stereotype individuals* strictly by the characteristics presented in the respective chapters. For example, after reading the chapter concerning the Asian/Pacific Islanders, do not conclude that all such persons are reserved and shy because this is simply not the case. Presented

---

here are *generalized* characteristics that may or may not be true of particular individuals within that cultural group. Thus, it is important to treat and respond to *individuals as individuals*, regardless of his/her culture, and to avoid stereotypic generalizations of particular people as you work toward better communication with respective members.

Chapter V

African Americans: Communication Styles and their Affect on Intercultural Communication

by Eugia M. Littlejohn and
Saundra B. Henderson

Eugia M. Littlejohn, M.Ed. Ed.S. is a native of Homestead, Florida and has long been interested in the interpersonal communication styles of African Americans. She is currently a doctoral student in Counseling Psychology at Ohio State University and is conducting research on the self-esteem of African Americans.

Saundra B. Henderson, M.Ed. Ed.S., a school counselor, holds both the Masters and Educational Specialist Degrees in School Counseling from the University of Florida. She is native of Ocala, Florida and is conducting research on the decision making patterns of Black high school youth and family influences on college attendance.

Introduction

Six humans trapped by happenstance
In bleak and bitter cold,
Each one possessed a stick of wood
Or so the story is told.

Their dying fire in need of logs
The first man held his back
For of the faces around the fire
He noticed one was Black.

The next man looking across the way
Saw one not of his church
And couldn't bring himself to give
The fire his stick of birch.

The third one sat in tattered clothes
He gave his coat a hitch.
Why should his log be put to use
To warm the idle rich?

The rich man just sat back and thought
Of the wealth he had in store
And how to keep what he had earned
From the lazy, shiftless poor.

The Black man's face bespoke revenge
As the fire passed from his sight.
For all he saw in his stick of wood
Was a chance to spite the White.

The last man of this forlorn group
Did nought except for gain.
Giving only to those who gave
Was how he played the game.

Their logs held tight in death's still hands
Was proof of human sin.
They didn't die from the cold without.
They died from the cold within.

Anonymous

There exist many discrepancies on the initial date that Africans were brought to the New World. Some reports state that Africans were brought to the Spanish colonies, known today as Haiti and the Dominican Republic, as early as 1505, 464 years before Columbus' arrival to what we know as America (Mintz, 1970). For approximately three and one half centuries after the slave trade had begun, and until the second half of the nineteenth century, slaves were imported into the Americas.

It is estimated by some historians that somewhere between 12 million and 15 million slaves were brought across the Atlantic Ocean and into the New World (Franklin & Moss, 1988; Mintz, 1970). These numbers are clearly higher than those of Europeans who immigrated to the Americas and of any other transoceanic travel having occurred during the seventeenth, eighteenth, and nineteenth centuries (Mintz, 1970).

In twentieth century America, African Americans comprise the largest minority group with recent decades having seen the increase in the African American population by approximately 69 percent. This increase is due largely to high fertility and high birth rates among African Americans. In 1980, it was estimated that approximately 26,480,000 African Americans made up 11.7 percent of the population in the United States. The trend is projected to continue at an even faster rate well into the next century.

Growing Up as an African American

It is not our intent to address African American history, lifestyles, past problems, racism, and so forth. However, before proceeding to address the issue of growing up as an African American in America, we wish you to consider a set of questions: *Need it be reiterated* that Africans (some were Kings and Queens in their own land) were brought to America against their will to be enslaved? *Is it necessary that we be reminded* that African Americans spent in excess of three hundred years in slavery? Are the blood stains on the battlefields, where Americans fought Americans, enough evidence that our country was divided over freedom and captivity of human beings? Can we forget those whose tortured corpses swung from trees because the skin that shrouded their lifeless bodies was of a different pigment? Is it possible to forget those who lost their lives in the struggle for equality and justice? Is it conceivable that one of the most powerful nations in the world today still openly discriminates against some of its own people?

The anecdotes that follow are not meant to portray African American life as bitter, but to convey the cultural circumstances under which most African Americans are subjected at some point in their lives. Consider for a moment the following accounts of our lives—both African-American women:

I was enrolled at a large, predominantly White Southeastern university and was seated one day in a classroom in which I was the only person of noticeable African heritage. The fact that I was the only *Black* in the class was not uncommon. Most African-American students at the university experienced that feeling of isolation at least once in their college career. However, this particular day the professor began to lecture on the assigned readings which had been taken from an anthology of short stories, one of which included Eudora Welty's "Why I Live at the P.O."

Several times during the lecture the professor mentioned the word "nigger," though the reading caused many of the White students to shift uneasily in their seats, it was considered appropriate since it appeared in the literature. At the close of the lecture, the professor made announcements of some events which he thought students might have been interested in attending and began by describing an upcoming lecturer as "mixed up" because she characterized herself as having multi-ethnic ancestry. Humored by some unknown thought after having commented on the woman's heritage, the professor began to sing a song about the "niggers and the Jews." Stunned by the lyrics of the song (the lyrics expressed, among other things, that "the niggers and the Jews" had no right being here, in America...) the students in the class gasped in disbelief. I was humiliated by the professor's insensitivity and was seething because of the personal affront that had been thrust upon me. Unsure whether or not I should flee the premises to show my shame or stand up and demand an apology, I sat and eagerly anticipated the end of the class period. After class I angrily confronted the professor and insisted that he give me an explanation why he had chosen to sing such a degrading song. The professor merely replied that he did not think it was inappropriate but was sorry if he had offended me. In tears, I left his office.

When fifteen, I arrived at school dreading the days ahead. Even though it was my second year in the "new" high school, I still hated it and wanted to return to my old school.

The intercom crackled with static and came to life with the principal announcing the news—MARTIN LUTHER KING, JR. HAD BEEN SHOT AND WAS DEAD. I couldn't believe it. For a split second, everyone was stunned. No one said a word. Then, everyone began talking at once as the students wondered aloud who had killed Martin Luther King and if the announcement could possibly be true. I noticed that, in this new, hated school where Whites outnumbered Blacks six to one, that the Whites appeared nervous as they also began to whisper among themselves.

During the next few minutes, the school's administrators met and decided that all Black students should be released from class to share their grief. The reason we were released was not so noble, for later I discovered that the Whites were afraid that the Black students would riot. What the administrators did not realize was that rioting was farthest from the minds of the young, rural, Black students; we were in a state of shock. No one had tried to help or ask if anything could be done to provide some means of comfort. Instead, we were left alone, feeling abandoned and helpless as we gathered in a small huddle and tried to make sense out of the day's events. Someone had a radio and we were able to hear the sketchy details available concerning the assassination. We understood one thing: a Black leader who had preached a doctrine of non-violence had been murdered.

Our feelings of abandonment were increased by the fact that the administrators could not find a way to communicate with us. One can speculate that they were frightened. Perhaps, some even sympathized with the person who had murdered the civil rights leader. Whatever their feelings, it is clear that on that particular day in a small, rural, Florida school, communication between Black and White racial groups did not take place. There was a lack of a basic understanding and a language to bridge the hurt and anxiety of the young Black students, who were frightened, and alone, and confused. The White students who were experiencing strong feelings were also ignored. The two groups were unable to reach out to each other as human beings during one of the darkest days in America's history.

The two illustrations above serve not only as painful reminders of the Black experience in America, but also as a reminder of a time when each of us was confronted with our own blackness. Not every African American's experience is as distressing as the recollections described, for often the blow of racism and discrimination are much more softened, and even supportive of environs and family. Though in recent times the African-American family has been under intense examination, it still persists as one of the greatest foundations of sustenance for its people.

Hill (1972) stated that many Black families have provided individuals with the strength to survive in oppressive environments. Black families have acted as stabilizers which have counteracted or balanced negative, dominant societal messages. A strong family can serve as an oasis in a cultural desert and can afford the occasion to learn the importance of our cultural strengths. One such strength which most African Americans are aware of, either consciously or unconsciously, is a rich, oral cultural heritage which has created a unique communication style.

As defined by Kochman (1981), "style" is an *attitude* expressed by individuals within a culture as exhibited by their choice of cultural form (i.e., language, music, dance). Further, Kochman (1981) stated that African Americans "prefer cultural forms that do not restrict their expressive capacities and the way they choose to express themselves with a given form" (p. 130). In short, Black style, whether related to communication or not, exhibits self-awareness, eloquence, power, vividness, passion, assertiveness and is more concentrated than the communication style of Americans in general.

Black English

Most cultures have their own form of language, and, as Weber (1985) wrote, so do African Americans:

> One's language is a model of his or her culture and that culture's adjustment to the world. All cultures have some form of linguistic communications; without language, the community would cease to exist. To deny that a people has a language is to deny its humanity (page 246).

Language is the product of one's ethnic or cultural identity and one's social environment (Lukens, 1978). Like many immigrant populations, Africans evolved a form of the English language which had its own linguistic nuances. This unique form of language, once known as "pidgin" or "pidginized" English, was maintained and passed down through subsequent generations to become what is known today as Black English or "ethnocentric speech" (Lukens, 1978). Black English is nothing more than a dialectical English that is spoken primarily by African Americans. Because this form of language fails to meet what is considered the standard form of English, those who speak it (i.e., African Americans) are considered by many as intellectually deficient. Weber (1985), however, asserted that:

> ...Black language usage stands as a political statement that Black people are African people who have not given up a vital part of themselves in slavery: their language. They have retained the cultural link that allows them to think and to express themselves in a non-European form. The ability of Blacks to maintain and sustain a living language, then, shows their control over that aspect of their lives, and their determination to preserve the culture. The use of Black language is the Black man's defiance of White America's total indoctrination. The use of Black language by choice is a reflection not of a lack of intelligence, but of a desire to retain and preserve Black life styles (248).

Since culture dictates the expression of language, communication is effected by culture. Communication, then, whether cross-cultural or intracultural, is not holistic in itself; it must always be explored in terms of the language being communicated and the culture in which the language exists.

Yet, culture is not the only factor that should be considered during the exchange of information, but many factors such as verbal and non-verbal cues must be considered as well. For example, in African American communication, identity may be detected through the use of familiar phrases or gestures, utterances, and/or dialects. As in other cultures, these cues serve as mechanisms of recognition. Verbal messages, however, are more readily discernible than non-verbal messages. Often interferences in communication happen when someone who is not a native of the culture, unwittingly breaks cultural rules of interpersonal interaction. It is not surprising that the most obvious affronts in cross-cultural communication are made when there are discrepancies in nonverbal signals. As you will read below, African Americans rely heavily on nonverbal behaviors to guide their interpretation of interactions.

Sample Communication Styles

While African Americans may use a variety of ways to communicate, it is important to discuss some notable ones. The importance of providing examples is to give the reader a view of the cultural underpinnings which influence the African American style of communication. They are *not* intended as vehicles for validating stereotypic beliefs. Hopefully, these examples will assist in better communication with African Americans.

Playing the Dozens

One example of expressive communication style in African American language is "playing the dozens." "The dozens," as it is called, refers to verbal competition consisting of insults hurled between two people. Historically, the term was used for slaves who were being sold on the market. If a slave had a disability, he or she was sold along with eleven other slaves who were also disabled for a total of twelve, or one dozen. Henceforth, the term "dozens" came into existence.

The following commentary described by a comedian illustrates a dialogue in which the dozens is being played:

Tony: *Hey, James. I heard your sister was so ugly they had to tie a porkchop around her neck just to get the dog to play with her.*

James: *Oh yeah? Well, you know they said they're gonna run the town drunk away from here. I guess your mama will be packing up her beer cans tonight.*

The cultural significance of "the dozens" is that, to a person of another culture not familiar with African American culture, it may appear to be an interchange which is cruel, aggressive, and the beginning of physical violence. Rather, the winner is the one who continues to dismantle the opponent through the use of poignant, humorously offensive remarks. Usually, an audience of listeners gathers during the interchange to hear the verbal insults and to determine the winner of the contest. The scoring is done by the audience through verbal comments which serve to excite both of the feuding combatants and encourage them to excel to greater heights. Weber (1985) stated that more than any other form of communication, playing the dozens "pits wit against wit and honors the skillful user of the magical power of the word" (p. 248).

It is important to understand this type of communication since on the surface it tends to support stereotypes that exist about the aggressiveness of African-American language. However, to the African-American community, the dozens is a high form of verbal warfare and impromptu speaking. It is a game, often played in jest (Weber, 1985).

Woofing

As in playing the dozens, some conflicts in communication styles can be attributed to cultural misunderstanding. This is true of the pattern of behavior called "woofing." Because of its similarity to aggressive behavior, woofing can be easily, and is often, interpreted in the same manner as a threat. A threat, according to Kochman (1981), can be defined as an "indicator of intent to act" in a manner that suggests bodily confrontation (p. 49). Yet, woofing in African-American communication patterns is distinguished from a threat in that it involves more of a trading of insults and a challenge to fight. There is an imminent exchange of verbal blows, however, physical violence is rarely a consequence.

The importance of understanding "woofing" as a behavioral pattern within the arena of cross-cultural communication lies in the level of aggression that it is assigned by persons of varied cultural groups. For individuals of other cultures (e.g., Anglo Americans), woofing may be perceived as an indication that physical violence will inevitably ensue. Yet, African Americans interpret "woofing" as non-violent and will often use it as a vehicle for settling arguments in lieu of fighting. This disparity in perception might best be explained by Kochman (1981) who asserted that African Americans and Anglo Americans have different levels of confidence in a person's ability to maintain self-control and anger at the verbal level without a resulting fight. Furthermore, where Anglo Americans have low levels of confidence in self-control, African Americans believe that they can maintain their level of anger at a verbal standing without it mounting to a total loss of self-control (Kochman, 1981). In the history of African Americans in America, maintaining composure, even at intense levels, was a learned and necessary evolutionary process for survival.

Rappin'

"Rappin'" is a form of African American speech which historically referred to the conversation between a male and a female. A pursuer (a male) "rapped" or conveyed (with the intention of winning favor) his appreciation for the object of his admiration (a female). As an example, in the movie *Color Purple*, one male character makes the comment to a female character, "Girl, you so fine, I'll drink your bath water."

This description makes rappin' seem like a classic case of cat and mouse. However, when this conversation style is actually witnessed by persons of different cultures, assumptions may be made about the occurrence of physical action as related to the comments in the dialogue.

The importance of rappin' as a conversation style lies in the fact that it can be misinterpreted by others from different cultures as a precursor to physical action. Rappin' is a form of verbal play among young Black Americans. In fact, in most cases it is not perceived to be dangerous, although it can be offensive to some females because of its sometimes sexual connotations.

Call and Response

There are other forms of African-American communication that are not at all seemingly aggressive. The "call and response" pattern is yet another form of expressive communication. According to Kochman (1985), call and response incorporates the elements of stimulus, structure, and manner of participation. It can be depicted by members of an audience or group responding to the "call" of a leader.

In most cases, the call and response pattern can be found in African-American churches where the preacher performs the "call" function while delivering a sermon and the congregation performs the "response" to the message being preached. The audience may respond in a positive fashion that can take the form of hand clapping or murmuring with remarks such as "Amen," "all right now," and "you better tell it like it is." This method of conversation is not limited to the church. Kochman (1985) stated that this manner of intercourse can be found in everyday expressive routines such as "giving skin" or "giving up the dap," the hand-to-hand exchanges in which African Americans sometimes engage. Further, Kochman (1985) asserted that African Americans' ability for intense and spontaneous emotional behavior provides for opportunities to accommodate free and uninhibited emotional expressions. The only condition for participation in such exchanges is that the level of expressions must be genuinely matched with intense and authentic feelings.

The pattern of call and response is important because it, too, is often misunderstood by persons of other cultures. Smitherman (1977) stated that African American speakers tend to surmise that, because of the lack of a response, White Americans to whom they are speaking are not listening. It is important, then, that dominant group members understand this mode of communication. Likewise, persons of other cultures who do not employ this convention may believe that when African Americans are responding in this fashion that they are rudely interrupting the speaker. The result is failed communication.

Signifying

Another form of communication used by African Americans is called "signifying." Signifying generally means intending or implying more than one actually says, rather than being forthright in inquiry (Kochman, 1985). In its relationship to asking for personal information, signifying can be used in an indirect way without insulting the person from which the information is being requested. The importance of this technique is that it may be used by African Americans as a "backdoor" means of eliciting information without using confrontive or intrusive questions which are not readily welcomed by many African Americans. Persons of other cultures should be aware that requests for personal information may be met with silence or with additional efforts to avert other attempts. This is especially true if information is sought in the form of probing questions. Even if such questions are asked quite innocently without the intent of prying, they may be misconstrued by some members of this cultural group.

To elucidate further, if a woman wanted to find out what type of job her male suitor held, she might comment, "My, that's a mighty fine house you have. You must own a bank, right?" Kochman (1985) explained that in some instances African Americans may hear these questions as hints for more personal information. These are only attempts at getting more information; this method is not a certainty. African Americans also may not choose to disclose personal information because they are not often sure how it will be used. History has taught them to be cautious of what they disclose in conversation. It is a belief that, since they have no real control over the distribution of the information given, it may be used against them. While some persons of other cultural groups may label this as "Black paranoia," African Americans have learned through experience that it is better to be cautious and withhold information to avoid personal and community exploitation. Clearly, effective communication will be difficult, if not impossible, to achieve in an atmosphere of mistrust.

Communication processes are often shaped and dictated by the willingness of persons from different cultures to engage in interaction. However, many attempts to communicate are foiled due to differences in the way messages are sent and received. Assumptions are often made that the messages that are sent are the same ones that are received. However, in cross-cultural communication this is often not the case. Historically, establishing and maintaining communication between African Americans and Anglo Americans has been especially difficult. On the one hand, each group believes that the messages sent are clear, since in the United States they purportedly speak the same language. These same messages, on the other hand, are sent through the use of communication styles which are often a result of the specific culture of the sender. They are then filtered and processed through the cultural screen of the receiver. Each cultural group has different and unique communication styles which are often misunderstood and misinterpreted by other cultural groups. Specifically, African Americans have communication styles which, when taken out of context, may easily be misinterpreted as violent, loud, and harsh. But, if an attempt is made to understand the cultural meaning and basis for these styles, a better understanding and more effective communication will occur. Revealing a condescending attitude toward Black Americans and/or "mocking" their respective communication styles, can result in mistrust and a breakdown in communication.

Barriers to Communication

A young, African-American college administrator and an older, White-American administrator were engaging in social chit chat while at an office gathering. A newcomer, another African-American administrator, joined them and introductions were made. The White administrator introduced her younger colleague to the newcomer.

"I want you to meet my colleague, Sally. She was also born here in Florida. It seems we who are native Floridians are becoming fewer in number each year in this area. Yes, we Florida 'crackers' must stick together."

The newcomer and the other African-American administrator were stunned for a minute and then began to chuckle heartily. The White administrator laughed, too, but was puzzled by their reaction. She soon made an excuse to leave the group, feeling somewhat uncomfortable but not really knowing why.

This incident illustrates how even honest attempts at communication are prevented due to cultural barriers in filtering information. The African-American administrators had found humor in being referred to as "crackers", which they interpreted as meaning poor Whites. Their White colleague, however, used the term "cracker" to describe a person who was born in Florida. In her estimation, it was a term used with pride since in many parts of Florida there are few native born Floridians left.

In the above anecdote, each of the cultures represented had their own definition of the word "cracker." Though people share the same geographical location (i.e., country, state, city, town, and so forth), dress similarly, and speak, basically, the same language, different cultures within that location have culture-specific idiosyncrasies. Furthermore, in terms of cross-cultural communication, this example illustrates that though African Americans and Anglo Americans share the same country, there are often differences in how the two cultures communicate and interpret information. We need more actual cognitive knowledge of each other's culture values and ways.

To assume that common outward appearances and even the usage of a common language create cultural similarity is a false premise. Barna (1988) noted that this phenomenon of "assumed similarity" can become a barrier to intercultural communication. The barrier or stumbling block is erected because, even though individuals *seem* similar, one should not assume that they are. Most likely there will be differences in underlying beliefs, non-verbal communication styles (i.e., smiles, nods, interpersonal distance, and so forth) as well as thoughts and feelings. Therefore, to assume that all of these areas are similar to one's own culture creates obstacles in communicating. When not sure, genuinely ask for more information or clarification.

One can readily see how if the concept of "assumed similarity" is applied to African Americans, the potential for barriers in interpersonal communication is even greater. Throughout history, African Americans and Anglo Americans have become acculturated to many of each others' customs. Though there are appreciable similarities between the two cultures, it should be remembered that they are distinctly different. It is up to each of us to learn more about each other's culture and to respect the differences.

Another communication barrier discussed by Barna (1988) is language itself. Many research studies have undertaken the task of studying Black English. There have been wide range discussions, remedies, and defensive statements about the verbal skills of African Americans. However, many researchers assume that they understand the meaning of the language even though they may not always appreciate the variety of communication styles used. As Barna (1988) clearly emphasized, a barrier to communication is created when persons of other cultures assume or think that they understand fully the language used by African Americans.

Quite similarly, Barna (1988) related the "presence of preconceptions" as another barrier to communication (p. 326). African Americans have had to contend with negative cultural information presented in the media, in research studies, and in legal, educational, and social institutions. Terms which have been used by these entities in referring to African-American culture include "culturally disadvantaged," "culturally deprived" and "culturally deficient." A picture has been sketched of a race which has no culture, is violent, drug infested, sexually promiscuous, criminally oriented, generally unintelligent, and lazy. Such beliefs and notions about African Americans have been carried forward from generation to generation and have persisted for such a long time that they have resulted in very damaging stereotypes.

Stereotypes are often an excuse used for the purpose of refusing to deal with a person on an individual basis. Therefore, if persons of different cultures refuse to deal with African Americans individually, and collectively as a diverse and unique group, real communication cannot take place. Effective communication cannot take place between people in an environment where stereotypes and myths abound.

The fifth barrier according to Barna (1988) is the "tendency to evaluate." It would be fair to say, without any qualification, that African Americans have been scrutinized more than any other minority group in the United States. African Americans throughout history have endured social, economic, and educational deprivation and have been judged based on the standards of other more advantaged American cultural groups. Consequently, the African-American minority culture, because of its unique differences from the dominant culture, may be viewed as primitive or backward. Cultural bias, then, "prevents the open minded attention needed to look at attitudes and behavior patterns from another's perspective" (Barna, 1988).

Assumed similarities, language differences, preconceptions, stereotypes, and tendencies to evaluate are all barriers to communication. In addition, the presence of high anxiety is a potential barrier to cross-cultural communication. Because of the anxiety that is generated in multicultural communication, the potential for failure is greater than in intracultural communication. Anxiety among Anglo Americans, in particular, may be heightened when attempting to communicate with African Americans since the latter tend to rely heavily on nonverbal communication. This may make non African Americans uncomfortable which, in turn, may result in further obstruction of communication. Because the risks are great, many dominant group members may seek only to interact with "special" African Americans who appear to be similar in speech, educational level or social graces. When this occurs, not only are opportunities for sharing experiences and commonalities averted, but also communication is limited.

Recommendations

There are no precise measurements that can be taken to ensure that an attempt at communicating across cultures will be successful. These are some implications for those who are willing to venture into a cross-cultural experience in communication with African Americans. Aside from remembering what has been mentioned about African-American styles of communication and barriers that prevent communication, one of the first rules of effective communication is to be aware of any stereotypes you may hold or over generalizations you might have made in the past. Although the overall African-American's cultural context should be given attention, each individual should be treated uniquely. Secondly, it might be useful to develop an investigative, but not intrusive, attitude (i.e., a willingness to explore) the African-American culture. Also, one should be willing to accept not knowing all the answers and leave room for ambivalence. And, above all, be open to addressing the issue of "race" in a *genuine* fashion and constantly assess your own feelings about sensitive issues. The last and possibly the most important suggestion is to be "genuine" at all times. Anything less will be a detriment to open communication.

It is highly unlikely that death, such as that described in the poem at the beginning of this chapter, would result from lack of communication. Yet, the "cold within" has viable roots in the ways in which people attempt, or fail to attempt, to interact with each other. Instead of playing out the scenario of one of the characters in the poem, allow yourself and others to experience the warmth of sharing through facilitative communication.

References

Barna, L. M. (1988). "Stumbling blocks in intercultural communication." In Samovar, L.A. & Porter, R.E. (eds.), *Intercultural communication: A reader* (pp. 322-330). Belmont, CA: Wadsworth.

Franklin, J. H. & Moss, A. A. (1988). *From slavery to freedom.* New York: Alfred A. Knopf.

Hill, R. (1972). *The strengths of black families.* New York: Emerson-Hall.

Kirch, M. S. (1973). "Language, communication, and culture," *Modern Language Journal, 57,* 340-343.

Kochman, T. (1981). *Black and white styles in conflict.* Chicago: The University of Chicago.

Lukens, J. G. (1978). "Ethnocentric speech: Its nature and implications," *Ethnic Groups, 2,* 35-53.

Mintz, S. W. (1970). "Slavery and the Afro-American world." In Szwed, J. F. (ed.), *Black America* (pp. 29-44). New York: Basic Books.

Smitherman, G. (1977). *Talkin' and testifyin': The language of black America.* Boston: Houghton-Mifflin.

Stanback, M. H. & Pearce W. B. (1985). "Talking to 'the man': Some communication strategies used by members of 'subordinate' social groups." In Samovar, L.A. & Porter, R.E. (eds.), *Intercultural communication: A reader* (pp. 236-244). Belmont, CA: Wadsworth.

Weber, S. N. (1985). "The need to be: The socio-cultural significance of black language." In Samovar, L.A. & Porter, R.E. (eds.), *Intercultural communication: A reader* (pp. 244-253). Belmont, CA: Wadsworth.

Questions for Discussion and Reflection

1. Describe a "typical" African American's communication style and your own communication style. How do the two differ? How might these differences affect your communication with one another?

2. Several barriers to effective communication are given in this chapter. Add three additional barriers that you are aware of and indicate how these might impede communication.

3. Assume that you are an African American and that you have been asked to write a theme titled; *The African American's Allegiance to Plymouth Rock.* Outline your theme.

4. Assume that you are a member of the American majority culture. What stereotypes are you aware of concerning African Americans? List 5 and indicate how such stereotypes might affect interpersonal communication between African Americans and majority participants.

Chapter *VI*

Cultural Perspectives in Communicating with Asian/ Pacific Islanders

by Mary Fukuyama, Ph.D. and Chikako Inoue-Cox, Ph.D.

Mary A. Fukuyama, Ph.D. is a Counseling Psychologist in the counseling center at the University of Florida. Dr. Fukuyama's father, a Japanese American born in the United States, was interned during World War II at Minidoka Relocation Center in Idaho. Dr. Fukuyama's professional interests are in multicultural counseling and the integration of the "mind-body-spirit."

Chikako Inoue-Cox, Ph.D., Senior Staff Psychologist in the Department of Counseling and Consultation Service at The Ohio State University, was born and raised in Osaka, Japan. She is Past President and Co-Founder of the Ohio Association for Multicultural Counseling and Development. Her research interests include multicultural counseling and women's issues.

Asian Is Not Oriental

ASIAN
is not
Oriental
head bowed, submissive, industrious
model minority
hard working, studious
quiet

> ASIAN
> is not being
> Oriental,
> Lotus blossom, exotic passion flower
> inscrutable

> > ASIAN
> > is not talking
> > Oriental,
> > ahh so, ching chong chinaman
> > no tickee, no washee

ORIENTAL
is a white man's word.
Oriental is jap, flip, chink, gook
it's "how 'bout a backrub mama-san"
it's "you people could teach them niggers
and mexicans a thing or two
you're good people
none of that hollering' and protesting"

> Oriental is slanty eyes, glasses, and buck
> teeth
> Charlie Chan, Tokyo Rose,
> Madam Butterfly
> it's "a half hour after eating chinese food
> you're hungry again"
> it's houseboys, gardeners, and laundrymen

> > Oriental is a fad; yin-yang, kung fu
> > "say one of them funny words for me"
> > Oriental is downcast eyes, china doll
> > "they all look alike."
> > Oriental is sneaky
> > Oriental
> > is a white man's word.

WE
are not Oriental.
we have heard the word all our lives
we have learned to be Oriental
we have learned to live it, speak it,
play the role,
and to survive in a white world
become the role.
The time has come
to look at who gave the name.

Anonymous (1989)

An old-fashioned stereotype of Asian/Pacific Islanders was that they were "inscrutable Orientals," mysterious, unfathomable, and that it was impossible to know what they were thinking. As more becomes known about cross-cultural communication, what was once "inscrutable" can now be understood as cross-cultural miscommunication. Asian/Pacific Islanders have been subjected to many stereotypes, as is so eloquently presented in the poem above. The label "Oriental" has often become associated with these negative images, hence the terms Asian American or Asian/Pacific Islander are the preferred terms for peoples of Asian and Pacific Islander ethnicity. In this chapter we describe Asian/Pacific Islanders (APIs), a composite of many ethnic cultures, and discuss some cross-cultural communication issues which can occur with APIs in the context of everyday life in the United States.

Asian/Pacific Islanders:
A Composite of Many Ethnic Cultures

Asian/Pacific Islanders come from a diversity of ethnic cultures, including Asian Indian (India), Pakistani, Chinese, Thai, Japanese, Filipino, Vietnamese, Lao, Cambodian, Hmong (Southeast Asian), Pacific Islanders (e.g., those from Hawaii, Samoa, or Guam), Korean, and more. Included are recent immigrants, refugees, long-time residents, and American citizens who are descendants of APIs. Consequently, APIs represent a wide range of socio-economic and educational backgrounds.

Although generalizations are made about APIs, it is important to recognize that many variations exist *between* and *within* the various ethnic groups among APIs. In this section, some of the demographics, cultural values, identity development, and myths and stereotypes of APIs are described.

Demographics

APIs are one of the fastest growing minority groups in the United States, and they currently comprise 44% of the total annual immigration, about 264,000 per year (Wong, 1986). Census figures in 1980 included 3.5 million APIs; by 1985 this figure had increased to 5.1 million, and has undoubtedly increased since. This rapid growth may be attributed to both immigration and refugee arrivals in this country. Since the abolition of the 1965 Immigration Act (which rescinded the national-origins quota system), there have been more opportunities for APIs to immigrate. The reunification of Asian families who had members with U.S. citizenship has been given priority since 1980. Also, individuals who worked in certain occupations have been favored, such as scientists, artists, or occupations for which there was great labor demand. For example, 19% of Asian Indian immigrants in 1975 entered under an occupational preference category (Hsia & Hirano-Nakanishi, 1989).

The demographics on APIs suggest important sociological variables which influence communication patterns. In 1980, the proportion of *foreign-born* APIs ranged from 28.4% for Japanese Americans to 90.5% for Vietnamese, with an average of 62.1% for all Asian groups. This is in contrast with 6.2% foreign-born for the general U.S. population. Consequently, the majority of APIs must learn a new language and make cultural adjustments. It also is estimated that half of all Southeast Asians in the U.S. are under the age of 18 (Rumbaut & Ima, 1988). Therefore, to fully appreciate the API experience, the complexities of "normal" development interrupted by immigration and acculturation into a new society for immigrants/refugees must be considered.

It is also important to recognize that there are many adjustment issues *within* ethnic groups, depending upon factors such as length of time in the U.S., immigration from a region which was at peace or at war, socioeconomic status in the country of origin, and transferability of skills and credentials. For example, 1975 arrivals from Viet Nam tended to be educated, urban, and middle-to-upper class, and generally adjusted well within the U.S. The more recent Vietnamese "boat people," however, suffered much trauma in getting to and adjusting in this country. Many came from lower socioeconomic backgrounds. In particular, teenage refugee youth who arrived with little previous education had more difficulties adjusting to high school than younger refugee students (Rumbaut & Ima, 1988).

The latest API arrivals, over 800,000 Southeast Asian refugees-turned-immigrants, have many needs, including those related to issues of poverty and economic survival (Gould, 1988; Hsia & Hirano-Nakanishi, 1989). Imagine the communication difficulties of rural, illiterate peoples who have been displaced by war, and then thrown into the midst of U.S. modern society!

Cultural Values

Historically, most Asian societies were structured with well-defined role expectations, such as patriarchal family structures. Within those structures communication patterns flowed vertically from parent to child, superior to subordinate. The values of "filial piety," or respect for authority, parents and ancestors, and protecting the family name were time-honored customs. APIs thus have had favorable views toward authority. Typically, APIs wanted to live up to the expectations of their superiors, and have valued obedience to rules and regulations. In this value system, individual strength was based upon group strength, and it was not unusual to subordinate personal wishes to those of the family or community. The typical API defined feelings and actions in relation to others rather than in individualistic terms. A case example of a young Korean college student illustrates the types of conflicts which can be felt between traditional Asian parents and American-born children.

> Kim was a 19-year-old second generation Korean American female student. She always wanted to be an artist and had exceptional artistic talents. Her parents were proud of the awards she received for her art, but they did not approve her choosing fine arts as a major when she entered college. Because Kim was the oldest child and knew how hard her parents had worked to make it in the U.S., she reluctantly decided to major in business, hoping "to make a lot of money to support the family." She acknowledged the practicality of a business degree, and expressed interest in law school. Pursuing art seemed to be selfish and only served her personal needs. However, she felt jealous of her American friends who were art majors, and who did not have family obligations. Kim's friends noticed that she was feeling depressed. She also experienced sudden outbursts of anger, breaking dishes and destroying her paintings.

The case of Kim demonstrates the possible value conflicts and difficulties in cross-cultural communication, in this case even within the immigrant family.

Asian cultures have been described as "shame" cultures. The socialization of children (and consequently adults) was shaped by inducing shame or guilt (Nakane, 1970). The fear of shame controlled behavior, particularly to "save face" and to "protect the family name." Filipinos, for example, have a special word for shame, "hiya," and a saying that "to excel is to shame one's friends" (Duff & Arthur, 1973, p. 207). The Japanese word "hazukashi" means shy, and implies that how one is seen by others is important because "others will laugh at you" (Kitano, 1973).

API's self-control of feelings was another highly valued characteristic. The Japanese referred to the suppression of emotions as "gaman." Such a strongly felt value was reflected in phrases such as "kiga chiisai," meaning "your spirit is small," in reference to psychological problems (Mass, 1976, p. 162). Suffering in silence, endurance, and self-restraint were seen as strengths of character. Self-control also was a necessity to preserve harmony within the family, again sacrificing individual desires for the larger group. Self-control also becomes evident in nonverbal behaviors, such as when an API shows little facial expression or other physical gestures. In addition, feelings of obligation and loyalty control actions. The Filipino phrase "ntang na loob," referring to a debt of prime obligation, is a set of reciprocal obligations especially felt toward the family (Duff & Arthur, 1973). This pattern of obligation can be seen in patterns of employment wherein the employee works for an employer from "cradle to grave" (Rohlen, 1974).

API families have emphasized the importance of education as a way to achieve success (especially in the U.S.), although there are some exceptions for specific ethnic groups. For example, among the Hmong, education is stressed more for males than for females, who are expected to fulfill traditional roles in the home. The importance of education to a Vietnamese youth is illustrated in a testimonial presented at an East Coast conference on education (Tran, 1984):

> During my five year stay in USA, I had some quite unsettling experiences.... The unsatisfactory programs and system of schools were completely unlike those back in Saigon. The institution there which I had long attended was strictly for boys, where manner, uniforms, responsibility and regulation were required. It's chaos in an American school as students came to school swearing at their teachers and did nothing. They had sex and drank and smoked; they are mannerless and unpatriotic. My few negative experiences in associating with Americans taught me one thing: Foreigners are not wanted

here. In school, a friendly conversation with native students could end up in a losing battle, as they started cynically to tease and intimidate us; they endlessly ridiculed our names, religion, race, language, physical appearance, culture, and most painfully, our parents, but we were very sensitive and most Vietnamese were just not very patient. Brawls often led to eternal street ambushes and cafeteria rumbles. Most poor immigrants and refugees were so much more responsible, polite, progressive, and intelligent in classes. This aroused American jealousy and more fighting resulted (pp. 31-32).

Interestingly, a study of Southeast Asian youth in San Diego showed that more "Americanized" youth were lower on measures of attainment of academic achievement than their less acculturated peers (Rumbaut & Ima, 1988).

Identity Development

API identity development may take several paths. For immigrant adults, their primary identities likely relate to the "old country." This first generation may be described as "traditional" if they adhere to Asian values and customs (Sue, 1990). Their primary rules for communication, therefore, are based upon traditional norms. However, the children of immigrants born in the old country who were raised in the United States may be described as the "1.5" generation (Rumbaut & Ima, 1988). These young people live in a bicultural world, between parental and traditional Asian cultural values and the culture of the United States in which they were raised. They may adapt two types of communication, one based on the values and language of their parents, and another based upon American culture and their peers. Second generation APIs born in this country of immigrant or refugee parents experience a bicultural reality depending upon the extent to which they acculturate in relation to their parents' acculturation. A bicultural pattern of adjustment includes preserving traditional values and beliefs while acquiring new values and practices necessary for success in the new culture (Randall-David, 1989).

The third generation may be more fully acculturated into American society, and at the same time show interest in their cultural origins, which is known as the "Hansen effect" (Hansen, 1952). The values systems and cultural identities of APIs influence the types of communication patterns used, and very often these factors operate at the subconscious level.

Generally, APIs identify themselves by specific ethnic group first, such as Japanese American, Chinese American, or Filipino, and secondarily with the broader label "Asian/Pacific Islander."

Myths and Stereotypes

In addition to cultural variables found within API ethnic groups, perceptions of API communication patterns are influenced by stereotypes held by the American majority. In the late 1800s and early 1900s, Orientals were described in derogatory terms, such as "heathens," or "the Yellow Peril". The American media also has portrayed APIs in degrading stereotypes (Quonset, 1976). Today, however, the term "model minority" has been used to describe APIs. This stereotype suggests that APIs have overcome racism and discrimination, and have "made it" in the U.S. (Suzuki, 1989). The *stereotype* of a model minority person is one in which the individual achieves high academic and economic status through hard work, uncomplaining perseverance, and quiet accommodation. In recent years, particularly with the international economic successes of Asian countries, APIs have been portrayed as highly successful, in "outwhiting the Whites," at the "top of the class," and over-represented in the elite institutions of higher education in the U.S. This portrayal of the "success story of one minority group in the U.S." unfortunately has fostered negative effects for APIs as well as for other ethnic minority groups. Initial reactions to this image, which first appeared in the 1950s, were flattering and positive for APIs. However, the sociocultural reality of APIs in the U.S. today is much more complex than the model minority image would suggest. The success image of APIs has been used by the media to discredit the protests and demands of more vocal minority groups. Furthermore, this stereotype has fueled ethnic conflicts among minority groups and reinforced increasing anti- API behavior (Suzuki, 1989), especially from other American ethnic minority groups.

Contrary to the model minority image, many APIs are far from realizing the American dream. There continues a long history of racism and discrimination against APIs, particularly against recent immigrants (Chew & Ogi, 1987). API scholars have concluded that the model minority stereotype is inaccurate, misleading, and a gross over-generalization (Suzuki, 1989).

The model minority myth affects APIs both internally and externally. When this stereotype is internalized, APIs may restrict their beliefs about "who they are" and consequently act out stylized roles. They also may be self-conscious in expressing themselves. Such "internalized oppression" then affects their communication styles. When this myth is externalized, it influences institutional (including both covert and overt) discrimination in education, training, and work force settings. For example, employers may (erroneously) assume that APIs are content in their employments statuses because they do not complain, and therefore overlook them for promotions.

Historically, API immigrants have been scapegoated during times of economic crisis. Commonly espoused negative attitudes toward API immigrant workers during the 1980s were strikingly similar to those expressed a century earlier when Congress passed the 1882 Chinese Exclusion Act to prevent Chinese workers from entering the U.S. These negative attitudes persisted despite that fact that during the early 1980s most API immigrants took jobs that White workers had turned down. Anti-API scapegoating also has fueled the growing rise in violence against APIs. For example, in 1982, Chinese American Vincent Chin was killed by an unemployed auto worker in Detroit as a result of his rage at the Japanese auto industry. On Christmas eve, 1986, arsonists burned a house sheltering 28 Cambodian immigrants in Revere, Massachusetts. In 1984-85, there was a 62% increase in anti-API incidents in Los Angeles county (Zinsmeister, 1987). The presence of APIs on University of California campuses has resulted in openly expressed prejudice such as graffiti which says "Chink, go home."

The racial character of the Vietnam War continues to be played out in acts of violence against APIs living in the U.S. Even though most Southeast Asians who settled in this country fought on the same side as the Americans, racist, anti-API attitudes which developed during the war have turned these refugees into the "enemy" (Kiang, 1985). For example, a racial incident near Raleigh, North Carolina resulted in the beating death of a young Chinese American man, Ming Hai Loo. In this confrontation between two White and several API men, the White men "expressed that they did not like `orientals'--especially Vietnamese" because they had lost their brothers in the Vietnam war (Anti-Asian Violence, 1989).

Increased public attention to the impact of Asian industries on the U.S. economy (e.g., success of Japanese auto industries and real estate investors) also has contributed to anti-API attitudes. General lack of awareness of the differences between APIs and International Asians, as well as of intolerance for cultural differences, also affect these negative attitudes. Anti-API attitudes affect *all* APIs, not just those of a particular nationality. For example, although the owner of the Chinatown Express Restaurant in San Francisco was born in America, to her neighbors she is still a "gook" (Kiang, 1985). Cambodians in New York are told to go back to Vietnam and Vietnamese in Ohio are told to go back to China. APIs who have experienced discrimination and prejudice while growing up also develop coping strategies which are evident in their communication styles.

Even a so-called positive stereotype, such as "model minority," has damaging effects. It serves the dominant culture by pressuring APIs to be compliant and conforming (Jo, 1984), and ignores the very real needs of members of this minority group. All of these forms of prejudice and discrimination negatively impact the psyches of APIs through lowered self-esteem and restricted patterns of communication.

In sum, the various stereotypes of APIs influence their self-perceptions as well as others' impressions of APIs communication styles. The stereotypes such as "quiet, good at math and science," or "kung fu/karate expert" do not do much to encourage or acknowledge communication abilities.

In reality, despite the differences which exist, APIs have similarities to other Americans. APIs have a heritage of survival under difficulties that come with immigration (or refugee status) in the U.S. APIs are achievement-oriented and rely upon the family for economic and emotional survival. Some APIs live in ethnic communities in urban areas (e.g., Little Tokyo or Chinatown) which sustain their cultural heritage and community bonds. Many immigrant and refugee families rely upon family businesses, although in some cases this can become exploitative when family members have to work long hours for few benefits (Bonacich, 1988). Nevertheless, APIs share many of the same dreams as other Americans: they work hard, make love, have family disagreements, and look for the best buys while shopping!

Cross-Cultural Communication Issues

Katz (1985) described the components of "White American culture" or "Anglo-American culture" as valuing rugged individualism, nuclear family, competition, mastery, rigid time schedules, and communication in standard English (with direct eye contact, controlled emotions). However, because there are so many different ethnic groups under the umbrella term API, it is difficult to generalize their many communication rules and patterns. Therefore, for purposes of discussion here, seven issues are presented which highlight key cultural differences between many API cultures and Anglo-American culture.

High Context Vs. Low Context Culture

API cultures have been described as high context cultures, wherein communication patterns are dictated by situational factors such as the age, gender, rank, and occupation of the speaker. A social hierarchy (superior-subordinate relations) determines who speaks, when, and how. In contrast, Anglo-American culture is a low context culture. People generally rely primarily on *words* to communicate, and are more likely to express themselves in the same ways regardless of the context of the conversation. Anglo-Americans have been perceived to love to talk "incessantly" (Loveday, 1986). Lack of the use of titles, using first names, and informality of speech may be seen as disrespectful by traditional APIs.

In a study which compared the use of personal pronouns (such as "I" or "you") in Japanese and English speakers, the Japanese were more likely to refer to themselves in a role (such as father, doctor, teacher, or big sister), while English speakers used the more personal pronouns "I" or "me." The use of titles associated with age and social position were indicators of respect and superior-inferior status (Suzuki, 1978). In addition, rules for the use of personal pronouns were determined by kinship lines in the Japanese family.

Potential communication problems in this area might include differences in norms of formality of speech. APIs might think Anglo-Americans are too informal in their use of egalitarian language. In addition, APIs might seek "status information" in order to know how to proceed in conversation, which may be interpreted as intrusive by Anglo-American listeners. An API will probably want to know age, occupation, or family status when talking with someone. In addition, do not expect instant "familiarity" with an API and be sensitive to contextual variables which influence the communication patterns. Be respectful of age and status.

Silence

Pauses in conversation and silence have different meanings to APIs as compared to Anglo Americans. Anglo Americans generally find silence to be uncomfortable, but APIs may use silence as a way to "think" while conversing, as well as to pay attention to the listener (Tantranon-Saur, 1989). Also, Japanese tend to distrust words and rely heavily on nonverbal communication. They may actually regard silence as a virtue and view wordiness as vulgar and crude (Kunihiro, 1989).

Potential communication problems necessitate checking out various perceptions of silence in a conversation. Speakers may be unaware that they are dominating a conversation if they are waiting to be interrupted to stop talking. APIs may think that Anglo Americans talk too much and are rude. Relatedly, speakers should pay attention to the "pause" points in conversation, and check to see whether the other person is finished speaking, or just thinking. Talkers can experiment with allowing more silence to exist between speakers (perhaps extend the silence from one to three seconds). APIs may have to learn how to graciously interrupt in order to express their thoughts in a conversation with Anglo Americans.

Direct Vs. Indirect Communication

Anglo Americans typically pride themselves on being honest and direct in their communication styles. Assertiveness is usually rewarded, and the individual is expected to take responsibility for self-expression. Direct eye contact and open disagreements are examples of direct communication. Conversely, Japanese typically value "knowing" through intuition rather than through direct expression. This indirectness fits with placing the group as more important than the individual; maintenance of group harmony often depends on indirect expression of feelings. Japanese rules of communication therefore follow a principle of cooperation and social exchange. In addition, indirect communication may be seen as a way of showing respect (Cox, 1989; Fukuyama & Greenfield, 1983).

Joe Wittmer, Ph.D.

Potential problems are obvious. More direct speakers may be unaware of how offensive or intimidating such personal expression can be. It is important for direct-oriented speakers to realize the power of nonverbal communication and to be sensitive to the impact of eye contact and other gesturing in interactions with APIs. Relatedly, APIs would do well to learn how to "hear" direct communications.

There is some cross-cultural advice from the Middle East, that the best way to get from point A to point B is *not* necessarily a straight line. Social conventions for conversations sometimes dictate that the communicators go in "circles" and loop around the subject several times before resolving or deciding upon an issue. We recognize that such looping may be confusing and frustrating for Anglos and others who are used to a more direct approach.

Personal Disclosure

Amount of personal (self) disclosure varies from culture to culture, and there are differences between "private self" and "public self" (Barnland, 1975). For example, Anglo Americans tend to be more personally disclosive and move more quickly in making friends while Japanese prefer to reveal less of themselves in public situations (Barnland, 1975). Thus, direct, self-disclosive approaches may be offensive to some APIs (Lanier, 1981). In contrast, APIs who are initially reserved (i.e., non self- disclosive) may appear to be distant or vague. They also differ in the depth of conversations (e.g., Japanese may speak less of their inner experiences than do Anglo Americans).

Unfortunately, there are many opportunities for personal offense under these circumstances. The easiest way to deal with potential problems in this area is simply to ask whether disclosures or questions are violating a sense of privacy. Second, allow adequate time for relationship building to occur.

Personal Space and Touch

Hall (1966) described cultures in terms of being "contact" or "noncontact" oriented in regard to use of personal space and touching. Communication in contact cultures involves physical closeness, occasional touching, and frequent gesturing, while in noncontact cultures, interactions occur at a distance which precludes physical contact (Herring, 1990). There is quite a variance within APIs in this regard. Asian cultures, in general, are considered noncontact, and formal communication is usually at some (physical) distance. However, norms in touching are affected by the situational variables of the interaction. For example, in some public situations, such as mass transit in urban Asian cities, there is a high tolerance for close physical contact (out of necessity).

The best approach to assess the norms for touch is to observe touching behaviors among APIs and/or with others from different cultures. Again, however, realize that the context of the situation may affect the norms for personal space and touch. In general, it is not appropriate for APIs to touch strangers.

"Saving Face"

APIs are likely to want to avoid a confrontation and to keep conversation harmonious. It is very difficult for an API to "just say no" when it might cause embarrassment for either speaker or listener. Consequently, an API may say "yes" as a way of saying "I hear you" and say "no" nonverbally or indirectly (through hesitation, ambiguity, or leaving the situation). In addition, APIs frequently use the phrase "I'm sorry." This is a way of saying "no offense intended," and should not be taken as an admission of guilt or self-denigration (Tantranon-Saur, 1989). In some API cultures it is also normative to smile or laugh to mask other emotions (Randall-David, 1989).

Another way of "saving face" for APIs is to maintain self-control and not make many facial gestures (i.e., keep a "deadpan face"). In refraining from facial movements, eye movements and expression take on more meaning. Direct eye contact is not comfortable for APIs, they may be more comfortable with fleeting eye contact. This communication norm to avoid direct eye contact may be one of the reasons why APIs have been described as "sneaky" or "inscrutable" by those who do not know their culture.

Speakers who want to attend to the issue of "saving face" will need to pick up on nonverbal cues to guide them regarding how much to pursue a topic in conversation with an API. Understandably, it is difficult for APIs to say when they are feeling embarrassed or ashamed. Giving APIs reassurances of good will are important, as is being willing "to own your mistakes." As APIs learn about communicating with others, they will need to allow themselves opportunities to learn different norms for conversations, and to take risks in new cultural circumstances.

Accents

For American-born APIs (or ones raised in the U.S. from an early age), it is offensive to be asked and told, "Where are you from? You speak English so well." The simple fact is that some APIs have heavy accents while others do not. Some people discount APIs with heavy accents, saying that they cannot understand them. However, understanding an accent involves the listener as much as it involves the speaker. A foreign accent requires listeners to "tune their ears" into the accent. Much as a translator interprets words from one language to another, good listeners translate certain sounds into specific meanings into their language systems. The greater the difference in accent from the sound of native speech, the more difficult it is to accept it (Loveday, 1986). Therefore, it certainly is permissible to ask for clarification. However, with practice in listening to intonation, it is also possible to learn how to understand an accent easily.

APIs are an integral part of the United States. Therefore, as the country's fastest growing ethnic group, it is important to be aware of the complexities of communication with them, and also of the "common ground" we share.

References

Anonymous (1989, Fall). "Asian is not oriental". *The Asian American Voice. A Newsletter for the Asian American Student Community at The Ohio State University, 1* (1), 15.

"Anti-Asian violence in North Carolina" (1989, Fall). *The Asian American Voice. A Newsletter for the Asian American Student Community at The Ohio State University, 1,* (1), 12-13.

Barnland, D. C. (1975). *Public and private self in Japan and the United States.* Tokyo, Japan: Simul Press.

Bonacich, E. (1988). "The social costs of immigrant entrepreneurship." *Amerasia, 14,* (1), 119-128.

Chew, C. A., & Ogi, A. Y. (1987). "Asian-American college student perspectives". In Wright, D. J. (ed.), *Responding to the needs of today's minority students. New directions for student services no. 38.* San Francisco, CA: Jossey-Bass.

Cox, C. I. (1989). "Acculturative stress and world view." *Dissertation Abstracts International, 50,* 04A. (University Microfilms, No. 89-13631).

Duff, D. F., & Arthur, R. F. (1973). "Between two worlds: Filipinos in the U.S. navy". In Sue, S. & Wagner, N. N. (eds.), *Asian Americans: Psychological perspectives.* Ben Lomond, CA: Science & Behavior Books.

Fukuyama, M. A., & Greenfield, T. K. (1983). "Dimensions of assertiveness in an Asian American student population". *Journal of Counseling Psychology, 30,* 429-432.

Gould, K. H. (1988). "Asian and pacific islanders: Myth and reality." *Social Work, 33,* 143-147.

Hall, E. T. (1966). *The hidden dimension.* New York, NY: Doubleday.

Hansen, M. L. (1952). "Third generation in America." *Commentary, 14,* 492-500.

Herring, R. D. (1990). "Nonverbal communication: A necessary component of cross-cultural counseling." *Journal of Multicultural Counseling and Development, 18,* 172-179.

Hsia, J., & Hirano-Nakanishi, M. (1989, Nov/Dec). "The demographics of diversity: Asian Americans in higher education." *Change,* 20-27.

Jo, M. H. (1984). "The putative political complacency of Asian Americans." *Political Psychology, 5,* 583-605.

Katz, J. H. (1985). "The sociopolitical nature of counseling." *The Counseling Psychologist, 13,* 615-624.

Kiang, P. N. C. (1985). "Why the Asians"? *The Boston Phoenix, Section 1,* pp. 7, 36, 42.

Kitano, H. H. L. (1973). "Japanese American mental illness". In Sue, S. & Wagner, N. N. (eds.), *Asian Americans: Psychological perspectives.* Ben Lomond, CA: Science & Behavior Books.

Kunihiro, M. (1989). "The importance of language in communication: A Japanese viewpoint." In Fersh, S. (ed.) *Learning about peoples and culture* (pp. 81-85). New York, NY: McDougal, Littell & Co.

Lanier, A. R. (1981). *Living in the US.* Chicago: Intercultural Press.

Loveday, L. (1986). *Explorations in Japanese sociolinguistics.* Philadelphia, PA: John Benjamins.

Mass, A. I. (1976). "Asians as individuals: The Japanese community." *Social Casework, 57* (3), 160-164.

Nakane, C. (1970). *Japanese society.* Berkeley, CA: University of California Press.

Quonset, J. (1976). "Asians in the media: The shadows in the spotlight." In Gee, E. (ed.) *Counterpoint: Perspectives on Asian America* (pp. 264-269). Los Angeles, CA: University of California Press.

Joe Wittmer, Ph.D.

Randall-David, E. (1989). *Strategies for working with culturally diverse communities and clients.* The Association for the Care of Children's Health Family-Centered Care Grant (MCH 113793). Washington, DC: Bureau of Maternal and Child Health and Resources Development, U. S. Department of Health and Human Services.

Rohlen, T. (1974). *For harmony and strength.* Berkeley, CA: University of California Press.

Rumbaut, R. G., & Ima, K. (1988). *The adaptation of Southeast Asian refugee youth: A comparative study.* Washington, DC: U. S. Department of Health and Human Services, Office of Refugee Resettlement.

Sue, D. W. (1990). *Counseling the culturally different.* New York, NY: Wiley.

Suzuki, B. H. (1989 Nov/Dec). "Asian Americans as the "model minority": Outdoing whites or media hype?" *Change,* 13-19.

Suzuki, T. (1978). *Japanese and the Japanese.* New York, NY: Kodansha International/ USA Ltd.

Tantranon-Saur, A. (1989). "What's behind the 'Asian mask?'" *Our Asian Inheritance, 6,* 67-70.

Tran, T. D. (1984, April). *A teenaged foreigner's view upon social changes.* Presentation at the Fifth East Coast Asian American Education Conference. (ERIC Document Reproduction Service No. 253 607)

Wong, M. G. (1986). "Post-1965 Asian immigrants: Where do they come from, where are they now, and where are they going?" *The Annals of the American Academy of Political and Social Science, 487,* 150-168.

Zinsmeister, K. (1987). "Asians: Prejudice from the top and bottom." *Public Opinion, 10* (2), pp. 8-10, 59.

Questions for
Discussion and Reflection

1. What value differences would an immigrant youth face if she or he had traditional Asian parents while living in American society? How would these differences affect communication between them?

2. What does the term "model minority" mean? How can this stereotype be damaging to personal and professional (career) development for APIs? How does it affect communication with the American majority?

3. What are some examples of both historical and current acts of racism against APIs? What, in your opinion, is causing these acts of racism?

4. What are some cross-cultural differences in communication which may lead to cultural misunderstandings between Anglos and APIs?

5. What do the terms "high context" and "low context" culture mean? What are the differences in communication styles based upon this concept of culture?

Chapter *VII*

Cultural Perspectives in Communicating with Cuban Americans, Puerto Ricans, and Various Other Hispanic Americans

by Carlos A. Hernandez, M.Ed., Ed.S
and Diane Estrada

Carlos A. Hernandez, M.Ed., Ed.S., a doctoral candidate in the Department of Counselor Education at the University of Florida, was born in Havana, Cuba. His research interests include the impact of acculturation on the Hispanic family, particularly in regard to providing guidelines for therapeutic interventions.

Diane Estrada, an M.Ed./Ed.S candidate in the Department of Counselor Education at the University of Florida, was raised in Guatemala, Central America where her family currently resides. Her professional interests include educating others in facilitating intercultural communication and family counseling. Ms. Estrada is the instructor of a course on intercultural communication.

There are many channels of communication through which we send verbal and nonverbal messages. As children, we learned patterns of communication from our parents and respective environments which aided our ability to relate to our world. Through a complex process of distinguishing *important* information, we develop methods of communicating unique to our circumstances. In a global perspective, each culture acquires specific modes of communicating. Unfortunately, without proper understanding among culturally different individuals, miscommunication results.

As Wittmer has written in proceeding chapters, if we do not understand a particular culture's values and traditions, we cannot effectively communicate with an individual from that culture. Knowing the culture allows us to use appropriate communication channels. Thus, in this chapter, we address some of the Hispanic cultural characteristics which need to be taken into consideration in order to develop successful, positive, and effective communication with members of this culturally distinct group.

The Hispanic American Culture

Population Statistics and Growth

Hispanics are the second largest minority group, and the fastest growing subcultural group in America, probably due to a high birth rate and current immigration patterns. It is projected that before 2050, Hispanics will be the majority group in the United States. From 1970 to 1980, the population growth rate was 6.1% for Hispanic Americans, 1.8% Black Americans, and 0.06% for White Americans. U.S. Government population figures indicate that the Hispanic American population increased by over 53% from 1980 to 1990, to total approximately 22.4 million people, with estimates of "uncounted" Hispanics as high as an additional 12 million people (Time Magazine, July 8, 1991).

Hispanic Americans are composed of Mexican American, 62.8%; Cubans, 5.3%; Puerto Ricans, 12.2%; Central and South Americans, 11.2%; and other Hispanics, 8.5%. Some 90% of Hispanics are urban dwellers, particularly in New York City, Los Angeles, Chicago, Miami, and large Southwestern U.S. cities. The average age for American Hispanics in 1988 was 25.4 years for males and 26.3 years for females.

Approximately 28.2% of Hispanics are living below the (U.S. government's) poverty level. The average Hispanic family has 2.18 children under the age of 18, compared to 1.85 for all families. Over 10% of the school age children in the U.S. are Hispanic, of which 27% live in single parent homes. In 1986, Hispanics comprised 7% of the total employed people in America, but less then 5% were employed in "professional" capacities. For example, from 1977 to 1984, Hispanic-American faculty in colleges and universities declined from 1.7% to 1.4 percent.

Historically, various Hispanic groups have tended to remain separate in the U.S. However, since the 1970s, the various Hispanic groups have begun to emphasize the generalized Hispanic cultural patterns and similarities, many dating back centuries.

The Spanish language and Roman Catholicism are two of the oldest and most significant cultural bonds of Hispanics. These cultural aspects have a significant, dominant effect on the Hispanic worldview. For example, Hispanics are very religiously oriented. They also do not seek to be "independent" and in "control" to the extent common among Anglos. Rather, they view the world as nonmechanistic, hierarchical, and spiritual.

The "family" is of paramount importance to traditional Hispanics. However, this orientation is not as strong for Hispanics who have been acculturated into American society. The traditional Hispanic family has a balance of power. The father has power based on "respect," the mother based on "love," the children based on "being loved," and the grandparents based on "wisdom." Understanding of these four power bases, and how they result in the familial structure of the traditional Hispanic family, provide for understanding of the interactions within Hispanic families.

Hispanic Arts

Since the 1940s, the music and dances of Latin America have "crossed over" into the American culture. Among the most popular are the *cha-cha, bamba, conga, rumba,* and *salsa. Mariachi* bands consisting of violins, guitars, and trumpets also have become popular in the U.S. Latin music also is an important influence in popular music, most recently represented by performers such as Richie Valens, Carlos Santana, Gloria Estefan, and Los Lobos.

Latin American writing is often focused upon personal relationships, interactions, morality, and values. Much of modern day Hispanic-American writing addresses the problems of change, acculturation, and the family. It is represented by authors such as Tomas Rivera, Luis Valdez, Heberto Padillo, and Milcha Sanchez-Scott. From the diversity of the musical and literary compositions of Hispanic authors and composers, the vitality of a culture whose heritage stems from centuries ago, but is much alive today, can be experienced.

Hispanics have been in America since before the Pilgrims. Their traditions and activities have broadened the larger American culture. In addition, Hispanics bring a focus to the family structure. Hispanic food also is becoming an integral part of America, through popular sale of items such as tacos, tortillas, corn chips, and salsa.

A crucial issue today for both Hispanics and English-speaking Americans is how the Spanish language will be used with and/or integrated into the predominant English language. This issue, which has lead to heated and even legal debate, is currently in the forefront of state and national legislatures.

Your understanding and appreciation of the importance of the Spanish language to Hispanics will assist you to communicate better with them. For example, not being able to speak the English language correctly is no longer as important to certain Hispanic American groups as it was a few years ago, as many are not learning English at all. This phenomenon will, of course, add to the communication problem.

Growing Up in Hispanic America

Discrimination

Like many minority groups, Hispanic Americans have been discriminated against in employment, housing, and education. For example, "standardized testing" in school systems contributes to discrimination against Hispanics because most tests used are not sensitive to cultural differences such as Hispanic vocabulary and customs. Such insensitivity affects test understanding, comprehension, and responding among Hispanic examinees. In addition, standardized tests frequently are created, scored, and interpreted by the Anglo American majority, and minorities (e.g., Hispanics) suffer "consequences" of biased interpretations that often lead to being labeled (inappropriately) as underachievers or learning disabled.

Low self-concepts are prevalent among many Hispanic youth, often the result of discrimination and prejudice Hispanics face as they strive for self-affirmation and acceptance. Discrimination also is experienced by Hispanics due to differences in appearance (e.g., dark complexion), surname, and inability to enunciate properly some English words.

I recall vividly my high school days when my sister and I were the only Hispanics in a student body of over 1,000 in a small southern town.

We were singled out frequently because we were perceived as being different. At first, my sister and I viewed this "attention" as positive. Students would ask our names and purposely pronounce them wrong to elicit laughter from all present. We also were asked often to "say something in Spanish," which lead to the giggles of our classmates—we were their entertainment! We were also asked to teach them how to say "dirty" or "swear" words in Spanish, much to their amusement.

My sister and I attempted to "fit in" by excelling academically and in sports. Those were difficult times because not only were we trying to cope with our own adolescence, we were trying to understand the hostile environment with which we were being forced to deal. Teachers, perhaps because of not knowing how, did not offer special assistance or support. Our parents, who were struggling with the language and majority culture themselves, could not offer explanations or advise us on how to proceed. My sister and I grew closer together, each having to rely on the other for the emotional and physical support not available to us from others in our school environment. Looking back, I am amazed at the strength, courage, and flexibility we exhibited during those difficult times when our feelings were hurt and our self-esteem wounded. I will never forget the personal struggles we endured simply because we were "different."

Treat Hispanics as your peers and equals; as individuals, not as people who are "different." Do it genuinely. A condescending attitude may be worse than a prejudicial one!

Discrimination is hardest felt by Hispanic Americans in the area of economics as they attempt to gain financial security and a better standard of living for themselves and their families. Bean and Tienda (1987) wrote that economic hardships in America's private sector are especially prevalent among Puerto Ricans, Cubans, and Central and South Americans. Hispanic men employed in the public (i.e, federal, state, and local government) sector earn significantly less than their national origin, self-employed counterparts. For Hispanics, as well as for other minority groups, employment discrimination contributes to dependence on social services (e.g., welfare) to provide them with the means with which to live.

Social programs geared towards providing vocational and career education opportunities can better prepare Hispanics for jobs that create financial stability, increased self-esteem and worth, and less reliance on social welfare programs. For this solution to come about, however, educating potential employers regarding their cultural bias toward Hispanics must be done in order to facilitate growth and understanding of the diversity among various groups of people living in America. Employers will need to learn effective ways to communicate with those who are different and to better manage diversity if America is to be productive in the work place.

Intracultural Characteristics Across Cultures

The American Dream

The United States is often idealized and potential immigrants tell exaggerated stories of how everyone in the States has a house, a car, and 2.2 children—The American Dream! Thus Hispanic immigrants enter the U.S. hoping to have it all. Somewhere in their mind is the image that with a passport comes a package full of dreams!

A harsh realization is faced by most immigrants as they enter American society. No package of dreams is handed to them; the passport does not come with instructions on how to survive in an individualistic, achievement-oriented society—one so contrary to what they just left.

Try to imagine the frustration of attempting to communicate your dreams to someone who does not speak your language, understand you, or the culture from which you came! Yet, these immigrants are not seeking your pity; they simply desire understanding, empathy, and encouragement. They want opportunity and a chance to communicate their needs, goals, and hopes for the future.

With the disillusionment of the new society comes the idealization of the old one. Many immigrants who talk wistfully of their homeland, remembering the good times, are told bluntly, "If things are so great there, why don't you go back?" This confrontation is frequently viewed as rejection or a form of discrimination. If they were to go back, they would realize that things were as they left them.

There is more freedom in the U.S. than from where most Hispanic immigrants come. This is especially appealing for Hispanic adolescents whose "individualism" is supported by their new peers. Translated to behaviors, these "acculturated" Hispanics place less reliance on family, the foundation of Hispanic culture. For traditional Hispanics, the family must always be together. Children are not encouraged to leave home prior to marriage, whereas in the U.S. the mainstream culture helps young people strike out on their own as soon as possible after completing secondary school. If you have a new Hispanic friend whose family arrived recently, be cognizant of the possible inner turmoil resulting from the clash of two very different cultures, especially where family values are concerned.

Adjustment to American society is stressful for both Hispanic parents and their children. Parents want desperately to hold onto their children and to pass on their Hispanic heritage and views of the world. However, children are caught between remaining loyal to their parents and their culture, and the desire to be accepted by their new American peers. They wish to be integrated into the majority culture, and yet maintain the values of the Hispanic culture. It is a difficult path to travel and causes frustration for both parents and children.

Raising Children

From an early age, Hispanic males and females are separated to play with same gender playmates. There are definitive differences in gender roles within the Hispanic culture. Boys are raised with fewer restrictions, and given more personal liberties. They can stay out later and go out with their friends by themselves, minus the chaperons so prevalent for females. A man's world is "out on the streets", where personal and family reputations are to be safeguarded, and "bread is to be earned." Females are raised to take care of the family and home; the home is their domain. They are never to be "out on the streets." They are raised to be soft, gentle young ladies (Acosta-Belen & Sjostrom, 1988). The Latino tendency toward extreme gender divisions, and male superiority, means that sex, the particulars of the male's employment, and the female's everyday culture are not ordinarily discussed between spouses, much less between parents and children. This is especially so in working-class Hispanic homes. Understanding this tremendous gender difference is essential if communication is to be effective with Hispanics of either gender.

The Hispanic female is expected to have a chaperon accompany her on each and every date. Most teenagers of dating age do not want, and are not required, to have chaperons, and to do so would probably bring scorn and ridicule from peers. For the majority of Hispanics, dating is taken seriously and expected to lead toward marriage. Dating is not viewed as a recreational activity. Conflicting views often lead to serious intergenerational and intercultural problems within Hispanic families. One very familiar question often asked by Hispanic parents, grandparents, and other relatives of their youth is, "When are you getting married?" This preoccupation can frustrate younger "American-ized" Hispanics who choose to seek a career before getting married, or who choose not to marry at all!

Traditions

Many Hispanic traditions are "adjusted" in order to survive in the American society. For example, while in many Latin American countries women remain at home to take care of the house and children, the high cost of living in the United States almost necessitates dual career/employment for Hispanic couples in order to survive. For a Latin male, this may signify failure to provide for his family, leading to low self-esteem and marital conflict.

For Hispanic females, life in *America* is a new way of being. She enjoys independence on one hand, but feels guilty about not being able to spend enough time with her children, about not being a "good" mother. A Hispanic mother, perhaps using a daycare center, experiences great personal guilt for leaving the children with strangers. So, whenever possible, Hispanic mothers try to leave their children with a family member. Many Latin American grandmothers take care of grandchildren while the children's parents work; such an arrangement is a typical expectation.

Conflicts in Communications

Different Dialects

While there is comfort found in small Hispanic communities within big cities, there are also some significant differences among Hispanics who are from different countries. Hispanics from Central and South America take great pride in the particular countries from which they came.

There also are cultural differences between peoples from different Hispanic countries, particularly for different Spanish dialects.

I am from Guatemala. When I first arrived in Miami, the Hispanic population consisted mainly of Cubans. I did not recognize the language spoken by Cubans as Spanish! Cubans speak much faster than Guatemalans and apply different meanings to different words and phrases. For example, Guatemalans use the word *sercha* to mean a clothes hanger whereas Cubans refer to it as *pechero*. Similarly, Cubans refer to a bus as *la guagua* whereas Guatemalans use the word *camioneta*.

There are also differences in worldviews between people from different Spanish-speaking countries. Therefore, if you wish to communicate effectively with them, it is important to know the individual's world view as opposed to assuming you understand them because you have taken a course on intercultural relations. Different Hispanic countries have different traditions, although all are very culturally rich and unique in their own ways.

Nonverbal Communication Styles

Keeping in mind that individual differences occur in all cultures, there are some nonverbal behaviors that appear to cut across Hispanic cultures regardless of country origin. Hispanics require a smaller personal space than do people from most other countries, especially Anglo Americans. They tend to sit and stand closer to people. They always shake hands in greeting, and after getting to know someone even slightly, tend to engage in an embrace, and/or kiss on the cheek (mostly between females, or male and female) greeting. Hispanics also tend to touch people to whom they are speaking. For example, they may place their hand on your shoulder while talking, or they may give you a quick pat on the back a couple times during the conservation. Eye contact, viewed as important by Anglo standards, is not maintained for long by Hispanics because it may be interpreted as a sign of disrespect. This is especially true when a younger person is speaking to an elder.

Superstitions

The Hispanic culture is unified largely by its religious beliefs, with the majority being Catholics. They have a strong faith in various saints, many of which are believed to "protect" them in different regards and situations. Some Hispanics however, hold beliefs beyond the Catholic religion, to the extent of being mystical. These Hispanics, particularly those from the Caribbean region, use fortune tellers and other mystics for personal guidance. They believe fortune tellers and mystics have the power to communicate with their "Guardian Angels," the ghosts of deceased relatives who watch over them. However, it is commonly understood, among the strongest believers, that one should never have a fortune told during a full moon!

The fortune teller usually concocts a special perfume designed to bring the visitor good fortune. Another favorite assignment given to the believers is instruction to take baths with rose petals and sugar for good luck. The use of herbs mixtures for medicine is also very common.

Some other common superstitions include setting a glass of regular drinking water by the night table to "clear your mind." A glass of water covered by a plate is placed upside down behind the front door in order to catch the evil spirits that try to enter the house. Children and adults often wear an *asabache,* or black stone, to keep the bad spirits away. An interesting and often practiced belief is that women should not place dolls or stuffed animals on top of their beds because it will bring bad luck into the woman's love life. While many Americans believe in the misfortunes of Friday the thirteenth, Hispanics believe Tuesday the thirteenth is their unlucky day.

The practice of these superstitious beliefs can be seen in the Rodriguez family. Mother Rodriguez believes she can communicate effectively with spirits and often consults a special mystic (fortune teller) to assist her in this endeavor. The family has been conditioned through the years to believe in "curses" and the existence of "evil spirits." Therefore, Mother Rodriguez keeps a glass full of water next to her bed, and if she finds an air bubble in the water (something she checks for each morning), an evil spirit has entered their house and bad luck is imminent.

One of us visited the lady with whom Mrs. Rodriguez "consults." The consultant, an elderly women, quickly offered to read "the cards" that would tell accurately of my past and future. I felt very uncomfortable, but also curious to hear her comments. The "consultant" gave very broad descriptions of people in my life. Although I'm a non-believer, I tried not to be disrespectful nor to insult her. Following the fortune telling session, she informed me that she could make a perfume which would "protect me from the terrible evil spirits and bring me much good luck" (for a small fee, of course). She also suggested I buy some jewelry which she had made herself. Wearing it would also be a "protective" device. I left the session with a very weird feeling.

Slang Terms

Common to most cultures are sensitive, yet distinctive ways of communicating by using slang terms. This manner of communicating is often handed down through generations. Its proper use is sometimes viewed as a rite of passage by Hispanics, especially in cases where adolescent males are taught by their fathers certain words that carry distinct, sexual overtones. For example, the term *papaya,* a fruit, is an Hispanic slang term for a woman's sexual reproductive organ. Slang terms are often expressed through jokes having sexual and/or derogatory undertones. Hispanic youth who have acquired these terms and phrases will sometimes use them to avoid having Anglos or others understand what is being said.

Gang-like groups also adopt their own Spanish slang terms, and often create new words and phrases to distinguish them from other, similar groups. The significance of this type of language is clear. The retention of Spanish in general, and slang in particular, is the most obvious, visible sign of retention of Hispanic cultural characteristics. In some extreme cases, the "refilling" of heavily Hispanic populated neighborhoods by incoming immigrants aides in them never wanting, nor finding it necessary, to ever speak English. Accordingly, use of Spanish and its associated slang terms is present and important among Hispanics, and serves to slow assimilation processes (Moore & Pachon, 1985).

Recommendations

To familiarize yourself with the Hispanic culture, you can review Hispanic literature, attend Hispanic cultural events, seek out and befriend Hispanics, or organize a Hispanic day filled with music, traditional dress, and food. These activities will help to acclimate you to the richness and cultural diversity of Hispanic Americans.

Keeping in mind that the overall Hispanic culture is comprised of many unique Hispanic nationalities, each having distinct cultural values, it is best to remember to individualize your conversation. This will prevent you from making generalizations about Hispanics that are individually insensitive. An initial period of friendly, informal conversation (i.e., chatting) before discussing problems helps to avoid appearing unfriendly or discourteous. In particular, genuinely inquiring "how is your family doing" is helpful in building rapport.

Allowing Hispanic individuals to define "personal space" parameters also is important for effective communication with them, and avoid prolonged eye contact during conversations. Make sure to shake hands in greeting; it is a sign of respect. Address older Hispanic individuals more formally than younger individuals, another method of showing your respect.

If Hispanic individuals with whom you talk do not speak your language proficiently, encourage and praise them for their effort to learn your language. Also, be open-minded in your interactions. Their customs and traditions may be different, but they are not bad or wrong. And if there is one thing to remember in trying to communicate with an Hispanic individual, it is that when in doubt, ask!

References

Acosta-Belen, E., & Sjostrom, B.R. (1988). *The Hispanic experience in the United States: Contemporary issues and perspectives.* New York, NY: Praeger.

Bean, F.D., & Tienda, M. (1987). *The Hispanic population of the United States.* New York: Sage Foundation.

Moore, J., & Pachon, H. (1985). *Hispanics in the United States.* Englewood Cliffs, NJ: Prentice-Hall.

Time Magazine, "The browning of America." (July 8, 1991), p. 17.

Questions for Discussion and Reflection

1. Discuss the difficulties confronting Hispanics new to America in acculturating to the American culture. What do you view as their greatest difficulty? Why?

2. When referring to the four power bases of the traditional Hispanic family, discuss how understanding them gives you an insight into the dynamics of the Hispanic family. How would knowing this assist in improving your interpersonal communication with Hispanics?

3. What are some of the traditional Hispanic customs that have influenced the American culture? In what way?

4. Discuss the Spanish vs. English language debate and how the different outcomes will affect how Hispanics and non-Hispanics will interact in the future. Should Hispanics be required to learn English? Briefly explain your answer.

5. What stereotypes are you aware of concerning Hispanic Americans? List 3 and briefly explain how such stereotypes would impede open communication with Hispanics.

Joe Wittmer, Ph.D.

A Brief History, Current Problems and Recommendations for Improving Communication with Mexican Americans

by Antonio Avila, Ph.D.

Antonio Avila, Ph.D. is a third generation Mexican American. His grandparents immigrated to Los Angeles from Sinaloa, Mexico in the early 1900s. Dr. Avila is currently a practicing School Psychologist in Gainesville, Florida.

Juan

John's real name is Juan, but the school he attends has changed it to John to accelerate his acculturation process. John's father has managed to escape the back-breaking work of the migrant laborer and find a menial, but less demanding job in the city. Unfortunately, only a few other Mexican American families reside in the area. John and the rest of his family speak only enough English to satisfy their basic needs.

John is dutifully placed in the local school in the grade appropriate to his cohorts. After two or three days we find his teacher speaking to one of her co-workers:

"May, does anyone on the staff speak Spanish?"

"Not that I know of, why?"

"Well, I have this little Mexican boy in class and he doesn't understand a word I say. I'm at my wit's end. I can't find any teacher or student who speaks Spanish."

"What are you going to do?"

"I don't know."

"Well, if I think of anything, I'll let you know."

We run into the two colleagues several days later. May speaks first:

"How are things working out with that little Mexican kid, Julie?"

"Oh, I don't know. The principal is looking into some possibilities for help, but he says we don't really have a program for kids like that. He's a quiet kid, and mostly just sits. He does like to draw, so I let him do that a lot. If he doesn't cause any trouble, I guess I will just let him be and maybe the problem will take care of itself. It is tough, though. The other kids won't play with him because they can't understand him either. They think he's weird. So do I."

Gloria

Maria had just arrived at her friend's house in response to a call. "What happened," asked Maria.

"It was his parents. He didn't even have the guts to tell me himself. His mother called and told me that she and her husband did not think that different races and religions mix, and that they just thought it better if their son did not go around with a Mexican Catholic."

Maria sighed and said, "Oh...[no]!"

"What is it, Maria, this thing about being Mexican? Why does it seem to make everything so hard?"

"I do not know."

"Does it last forever?"

"I think so, Gloria; I think it does."

Friends

Five boys were sitting in a restaurant having lunch. They resembled a group of typical Anglo-Saxon, middle-class teenagers. One, however, was not. He was a Mexican American. His name was Henry.

Four members of the group, including Henry, had been friends for some time, and the other three knew Henry was of Mexican descent. The fifth boy was a relatively new member of the group, and the heritage of the others had not crossed his mind.

As they sat, a couple entered the restaurant. The male could have been of Indian or Mexican descent because he had very black, long, straight hair and the physiognomy typical of Native American Indians and many Mexican Americans. The woman had blonde hair and fair skin.

"Damn! Will you look at that! Nothing makes me any more mad!"

The other four boys looked up at the fifth, and Henry asked, "What?"

"Seeing a beautiful white woman all hunched up against a greasy spic!"

The other four boys froze. Henry's three friends had seen him tear into many another boy for much less. Fortunately, though young, Henry was maturing and beginning to learn the futility of trying to beat prejudice out of people. He let it pass, but you can be assured that the other three friends soon clarified an issue for the fourth, and such an incident, in this group, did not happen again. (Avila & Avila, 1988, pp. 304-307)

The preceding passages are real life anecdotes which help to illustrate experiences common to many Mexican Americans growing up in America today. These experiences illustrate blatant prejudice and biases that greatly contribute to problems in communication. They result from failure to understand a unique culture and the unique difficulties facing many Mexican Americans as they try to survive in the larger American society. Lack of cognitive knowledge about the values, mores and/or ways of this distinctive group can add to discriminatory practices. In this section, I hope to sensitize you to the plight of the Mexican American in the 1990s and offer some recommendations for improving your interpersonal communication with this group of people.

An Historical Perspective

The Mexican American story began more than four hundred years ago on February 19, 1519, when Hernando Cortez, along with approximately 800 soldiers, 14 cannons, and 16 horses landed on the Yucatan Peninsula (Prescott, 1934). Within three years, this handful of men accomplished a seemingly impossible task. Cortez and his men were able to conquer an entire empire numbering millions of people. In doing so, they established not only a new nation, but a new breed of human beings as well. Many factors were responsible for the relative ease with which Cortez and his men toppled the Aztec empire; however, three stand out. First, Mexico consisted of numerous Indian tribes under the very loose control of the highly aggressive Aztecs. Many of those tribes had been conquered by the Aztecs, and resented their conquerors immensely. This resentment created disharmony among the tribes. When Cortez arrived, he was able to recruit large numbers of natives to his cause with little difficulty.

Second, although the Aztecs were civilized and highly advanced in many ways (e.g., they had developed an accurate calendar and practiced astronomy), they also were barbaric and considered crude. The Aztec armies consisted of foot soldiers armed with clubs, knives and swords. They had never encountered muskets nor seen horses, and were reluctant to fight against even a small army equipped with this novel, intimidating equipment. The explosions of rifles and cannon and the awesome sight of huge animals with armored warriors on their backs terrified the Aztec natives, causing them to flee in fear (Longstreet, 1977).

A third factor was an unfortunate (for the Aztecs) artifact of the Aztec religion. The Aztecs believed that a white, bearded god once ruled Mexico and would one day return to resume his reign. When Cortez arrived, many of the natives were convinced that he was that god, and either joined Cortez, or failed to resist him out of fear. The Aztec emperor, Montezuma, himself confused and unable to decide on the divinity of Cortez, made many mistakes and blunders because he neither wanted to surrender his nation to plunderers nor offend a god (Longstreet, 1977).

Given these circumstances, it did not take long for Cortez to conquer the country. Having conquered Mexico, the Spaniards began to interbreed with the natives, creating a new breed of human—the Mestizos.

The Spaniards did not stop in Central America in their search for riches and new lands to call their own, but also sent bands of priests, soldiers, and plunderers northward to the southwestern and far western portions of what is now the United States. As the Spaniards pushed northward, the people they encountered were, for the most part, rather primitive and unaggressive Indians who offered little resistance (Longstreet, 1977).

Over the years the Mestizos became well established in Mexico and what was to become the southwestern portion of the United States. What might be called the second phase of "Mexicanization" occurred at this point. The Mestizos decided that independence from Spain was in order, and war ensued. The war for independence did not come easily. However, the years of war left many Mestizos in a terrible state of poverty. Thus, seeking to improve their lives, thousands of Mestizos headed north in search of "greener pastures" (i.e., better living conditions).

Modern Mexican-American ancestry is difficult to determine in light of four hundred years of Mexicans interbreeding with Mexican Indians, American Indians, and Northern Europeans. As Torrey (1986) stated, it is difficult, if not impossible, to group Mexican Americans:

> Grouping together all Mexican Americans is simplistic and naive, for they range from braceros who come from Mexico to pick crops, to middle-class, activist Chicanos who are proud of their heritage, to wealthy, totally assimilated professionals who are Mexican American in name only. Nor do generalizations about the subculture take into consideration the facts that Mexican Americans come from different parts of Mexico, with distinct cultural differences, that they may be more Spanish or more Indian in their heritage, or that one group of "Mexican Americans" in southern Colorado came to the United States directly from Spain and were never Mexicans at all. Such facts set limiting boundaries on generalizations about the subculture, and these boundaries should be kept in mind (p. 132).

Their story has been that of a people seeking new and better lives. Unfortunately, the Mexican American experience has been for the most part disappointing, with very few actually realizing the dreams of a better life. Instead, they were treated and exploited as slaves. More recently, they have been segregated into America's ghettos and barrios, continuing to be exploited.

A Current Perspective

The American Hispanic population, of which Mexican Americans are by far the greatest number, is predicted to become the largest minority in the United States during the early 1990s. This proportionate growth movement will most likely be accelerated by a new immigration bill recently passed in the United States which allows millions of illegal aliens, many from Mexico, to become American citizens. At present, approximately 12 million Mexican Americans reside in the United States. However, some of their descriptive statistics are not encouraging (Carter, 1989):

1. One third of the Mexican Americans living in the United States live in poverty and are disproportionately represented in low income, manual labor occupations.

2. They obtain an average of 7.1 years of education.

3. They have a lower educational level than Blacks or Whites and a greater drop-out rate than either group.

4. By the twelfth grade, 40% have dropped out of school.

5. Only one percent go to college.

6. Mexican Americans have the highest illiteracy rate of any group in the United States.

7. Many are segregated in schools that are almost completely Mexican American.

8. Many are 2, 3, or 5 years behind in school.

This sad state of affairs—limited education, high drop out rates, illiteracy, and poverty—is not necessarily reserved for Mexican Americans. Most minorities, whether they are black, brown, red, or yellow suffer the same problems. Minorities in America are often oppressed, stuck in the dead end cycle of poverty, victims of prejudice and discrimination, and alienated from the larger society. However, there are some differences for Mexican Americans which distinguish them from other American minorities. Understanding these differences facilitates better communication with them. Such understanding is in fact essential for effective communication with Mexican Americans.

Some Communication Barriers

Language. Not knowing their language is an obvious barrier to effective communication with Mexican Americans because both Spanish and English proficiency vary greatly among them. Some Mexican Americans speak virtually no English; others speak virtually no Spanish; and the rest speak every possible combination between the extremes. Generally, the less English spoken by Mexican Americans, the more they will be subject to prejudice and alienation.

Few things can be more frightening and unsettling than to find oneself surrounded by people speaking a language one does not understand, such as if you are a young child who speaks only a little Spanish and are thrust into a classroom of 20 or 30 other children with a teacher who speaks only English. Such a scenario does not make for a very promising future for the child. Lacking the tools necessary to express even the most basic needs and being unable to understand others, the child becomes frightened, confused, isolated, and lonely. The other children in the class, in turn, may reject, ignore, or tease the child. The teacher is likely frustrated and confused, and may give up trying to do anything other than to find menial things to occupy the child's needs. As time passes, the Mexican American child may develop defenses such as withdrawal, aggression, or hostility, which are definitely not conducive to success in the larger American society or in its classrooms.

Migrant Worker Status. Compared to other American minorities, the migrant labor work force is comprised of a disproportionate number of Mexican Americans. Being a member of a migrant family carries with it many significant problems and hardships. For example, the health of these migrant families is generally very poor. Relatedly, Hernandez (1983) provided the following statistics for migrants:

1. Their infant mortality rate is 12% higher than the national average.

2. Their death rate from influenza is 200%, from tuberculosis 260%, and from accidents 300% higher than the national average.

3. The life expectancy of migrant workers is 49 years.

Migrant families move constantly, typically remaining in one place for only three or four months at a time. They have no place to call home, no roots, and no place to belong. Their possessions are limited to what they can carry in dilapidated cars or trucks. The living conditions of migrant families are often disgusting and they are terribly exploited.

Frequent moving has devastating effects on the ability of children of Mexican American migrant families to obtain a decent education. They are constantly trying to "catch-up" to their same-age peers, which is an impossible task when they are always on the move. These children end up acquiring limited academic skills at best, which creates a vicious cycle with little hope of escape from the migrant way of life.

Games People Play. The oppression and discrimination Mexican Americans encounter in America often encourages Mexican American individuals to go to great lengths to attempt to disassociate themselves from their own group. However, for some Mexican Americans, their physical features make such denial impossible. For example, the more a Mexican American resembles an *Indian*, the more *prejudice* and *discrimination* that person will encounter! This group of Mexican Americans may be the most discriminated against of any minority group in America, simply because of the way they look! Mexican Americans who do not possess the Indian features can escape many of the hazards encountered by those who fit the physical stereotype, and generally experience much less discrimination.

My father told me of an encounter of his, as a young boy growing up in East Los Angeles, illustrative of this problem. He had gone to the post office for his mother to mail a package on which was printed the family name, "Avila," (obviously of Hispanic origin). The postal clerk read the name, and in a friendly manner asked, "Is that your name?" My father replied that it was, and the clerk again asked in a friendly manner if the name was Spanish. My father, then young and naive about many things, replied "No, it's Mexican." At that point something happened which he did not understand until much later, after he had seen it happen many times. The clerk's attitude toward him changed drastically. The clerk replied, "Oh," and became cold and distant when only moments before he had been warm and friendly. The clerk processed the package with no further verbal exchanges. My father informed me that through later experiences he came to realize that people of Mexican and Spanish descent were not perceived similarly in the larger society. Being Spanish, it seems, was somehow *better* than being Mexican. My father discovered quickly that he could get a lot further by saying he was Spanish than by being honest about his heritage. Fortunately, as he matured, he later realized that it was easier to select potential friends if he was honest about his Mexican heritage. The "good friend" prospects were those people who displayed no character changes when he was honest with them.

Many Mexican Americans have learned to play the "I'm Spanish, not Mexican" game well in order to avoid discrimination. Others have gone so far as to deny both Mexican and Spanish heritage, and pass themselves off as Italian, Jewish, or any other nationality for which they think they can be mistakenly identified. This kind of self-denial has psychologically devastating effects on individual Mexican Americans because they soon come to believe they are inferior human beings.

How do you feel when you hear the term "Mexican?" Do you have a stereotyped, negative image of Mexican Americans? Do you view them as dirty? Greasy? Lazy? If so, it will be necessary to move beyond these images to communicate effectively with Mexican Americans. Such images translate into ineffective communication patterns.

The Mexican-American Heritage

Intercultural conflicts are a frequent source of frustration and alienation for Mexican Americans because many of their values conflict with those of the larger American society. These conflicts serve thus as significant burdens for the Mexican American and are the cause of much miscommunication with the majority American society.

The Mexican-American heritage is highly socialistic, with the family unit being of primary importance. The family unit takes precedent over all outside concerns, including school, work, and social matters. Cooperation is favored strongly over competition, with the latter being perceived as an insulting endeavor. Because of this orientation, many Mexican Americans enter the "competitive" American society favoring group rather than individual success, and thus find themselves out-of-sync with "mainstream" American values. And, if you are (or even appear to be) in direct competition with a Mexican American, for whatever reason, communication between you will be difficult.

The Mexican-American culture also is highly authoritarian. Children are taught to give unquestioned obedience to the head of the family and to be strongly dependent on that individual for decision making. As a result of this style of upbringing, many Mexican Americans are quiet and submissive. However, these traits should not be misinterpreted as sullenness or uncooperativeness. It is simply the way many Mexican Americans are!

The Mexican-American culture is characterized by orientation to the present and does not stress preparation for the future. Also, little importance is placed on acquisition of material goods. These two characteristics are, of course, in direct conflict with the "American way." Much miscommunication occurs because of this specific, culturally different life view.

Some Mexican-American males may have a code of honor which emphasizes the "macho" image and many consider themselves biologically superior to the female. The macho image is associated with the expectation that one suffers frustration and disappointment in silence, avoids "losing face" in front of peers, and adjusts to problems rather than making attempts to solve them. The result is an exaggerated ideal of "machismo" or masculinity (Torrey, 1986). This often lends to miscommunication with members of the majority society who do not (or do not want to) understand the Mexican American male "code of honor."

The status of women in the traditional Mexican-American culture, as in most Latin cultures, is clearly inferior compared to that of males. Women are expected to be submissive and to overlook the indiscretions of males. For example, there is a certain casual acceptance of men who "play around," but not for women who do so. Virility is measured primarily by a man's sexual potency. Obviously, in American society today, this is not well-received as a social standard, and is the cause for many communication breakdowns with Anglos and others. Torrey (1986) placed the role of the Mexican American female in perspective when he stated:

> Girls are valued primarily for their virtue, and an unmarried girl's honor is equated with that of the family. Young women are expected to get married, and the maternal role is very highly valued. Women are late to mature, often because the grandmother lives with the family and competes in maternal care of the grandchildren. There is

Joe Wittmer, Ph.D.

a concomitant undervaluation of the sexual and companionship roles of women; sex is prudishly accepted by "nice women" only as an obligation (p. 141).

Any Mexican Americans entering the larger American society with these culturally influenced orientations are clearly going to be in for difficulties. Relatedly, anyone wishing to open channels of communication with Mexican Americans must understand that these orientations are deeply ingrained in the Mexican American character and should not be challenged. To do so guarantees rejection and makes open communication with participants from this group virtually impossible.

Trying to Cope. In the attempt to cope in the larger American society, many Mexican Americans have developed self-defeating behaviors. For example, Mexican American parents often feel that they cannot give their children the skills necessary to cope within American society. These parents feel inferior to Caucasians, and thus go out of their way to avoid them. For example, it is out of fear and a sense of inferiority, rather than apathy, that some Mexican American parents will not come to school when their child is experiencing difficulty.

Similarly, they may not respond to questions from their employers or answer the door when a perceived authority figure comes calling. In order to communicate more effectively with the Mexican American, it is important that one be aware of this behavior and that it not be exploited.

Traditionally, Mexican Americans place utmost importance on family relationships. The "family" may include neighbors, owners of the small neighborhood grocery store down the street, godparents, grandparents, and close friends. The family is group-oriented, even in decision making. All members may have a say in adopting family rules and solving family problems. Thus, the family is often an extended one. In addition, the ideal family works as a team, with the focus on the good of the whole or the good of another. The emphasis on family encourages members toward interdependence rather than independence. Many of these families have the common bond of "carino," a deep sense of unqualified caring and protection. All family members are considered equal and accepted unconditionally. They are valued simply because they are, not because of what they have done or not done. A member is not usually expelled from the family as a result of unacceptable actions or attitudes (Prevention Review, 1991).

Many Mexican-American parents, fearing that their values conflict with the majority, refrain from trying to instill their own values in their children. Rather, they hope their children will assimilate the values of the majority through the schools and make a better adjustment than they themselves were able to do. Unfortunately, often that is not what happens. Instead, the children grow up without a clear set of values. They become confused, and they have just as much (if not more) trouble adjusting to the greater American society than did their parents. As a result, many Mexican-American children exhibit the problems of delinquency and academic failure.

Some Recommendations

Along with all the above, anyone desiring to communicate at the feeling level with Mexican Americans should be aware that emotions are to be suppressed in this culture, especially among the males. "Correct behavior" is important and failures and shortcomings are not easily admitted. Most relationships are characterized by emotional restraint (Torrey, 1986). The Mexican American, both male and female, grows up with a fear of his or her own emotions.

A sensitive attitude toward, and knowledge of, the Mexican-American heritage are important determinants of how well you will be able to communicate with members of this culturally distinct group. Unfortunately, Mexican Americans often are thought of as "foreigners" who must be taught the characteristics and values of the larger society, but at the expense of their cultural heritage. It is important to remember that Mexican Americans are not foreigners; they are Americans who have historical roots different from but not inferior to those of other Americans. Effective communication with Mexican Americans requires acceptance and respect for the rich cultural heritage of this group of Americans.

The purpose of this chapter has been to provide some insight into the plight of Mexican Americans and to provide some tips on how to understand and communicate better with them. However, it certainly has not been to suggest that they are all alike. Therefore, it is *important* not to convey *preconceived generalizations* in interacting with Mexican Americans. Such preconceptions will be obvious to Mexican Americans and doom your relationships with them to failure from the very beginning.

A caution is in order. The word "Chicanos" is currently a popular term used to refer to Mexican Americans. It also is often used by militant and/or poor Mexican Americans as a designation of pride or unity. However, the word "Chicano" is not perceived by all Mexican Americans in the same light. To many Mexican Americans, especially older members of that minority group, the word is distasteful, and conveys an image of the poor, uneducated, and exploited field hand. Eliminate or restrict your use of the term "Chicano." Mexican American is preferred because it is not offensive to anyone.

Be flexible and genuine when conversing with Mexican Americans. Use whatever communication techniques you feel will be useful in relating to them. But, above all, be flexible and do not be concerned about asking sincere, honest questions when seeking clarity.

You also are urged not to judge Mexican Americans by your own value system. Study and learn as much as you can about their culture, and make judgments from that perspective only.

References

Avila, D.L., & Avila, A.L. (1988). Mexican Americans. In Vacc, N., Wittmer, J. & DeVany, S. (eds.), *Experiencing and counseling multicultural and diverse populations* (2nd ed.) Muncie, IN: Accelerated Development, pp. 289-315.

Carter, T.P. (1989). *Mexican Americans in schools: A history of educational neglect.* New York: College Entrance Examination Board.

Long, S.M. (1982). "An American profile: Trends and issues in the 80s." *Educational Leadership, 39,* pp. 460-464.

Hernandez, N.G. (1983). "Variables affecting achievement of middle school Mexican American students". In *Review of Educational Research, 43,* pp. 1-39.

Longstreet, D. (1977). *All star cast: An anecdotal history of Los Angeles.* New York, NY: Crowell.

Prescott, W.H. (1934). *The conquest of Mexico.* Garden City, NY: International Collectors Library American Headquarters.

"Reaching Hispanic/Latino audiences" (July, 1991). *Prevention Review.*

Torrey, E.F. (1986). *Witchdoctors and psychiatrists.* Northvale, NJ: Jason Aronson.

Statistical abstract of the United States (110th ed.). (1990). Washington, DC: United States Department of Commerce, Bureau of Census.

Questions for
Discussion and Reflection

1. The failure of our society to fully integrate the Mexican American as a first class citizen is clearly in evidence in the 1990s. Assume you have been requested to make four recommendations to the United States Congress to assist in accomplishing this integration. What four recommendations would you make and for what reasons? How would your recommendations improve communication between Mexican Americans and the majority American culture?

2. What are the most pressing needs of Mexican Americans in the 1990s? Assume that you have been asked to interview a member of the Mexican American community concerning this topic. Develop a set of five questions you might ask which will enable you to obtain factual information from the person you will interview.

3. Assume you are Mexican American and that you've been requested to give a lecture on *"Heroism at the Alamo."* Outline your presentation.

4. In what ways have Mexican-American cultural values and ways been distorted by the American majority? Select three and indicate how this distortion might affect interpersonal communication between the two groups.

Chapter *VIII*

Cultural and Historical Perspectives in Communicating with Native Americans

by Patricia Stroud Reifel, M.Ed.

This chapter was written in collaboration with **Patricia Stroud Reifel, M.Ed.** Ms. Reifel, certified as Native American by the Bureau of Indian Affairs, is an Ed.S. candidate in Counseling at the University of Florida. Her maternal grandfather was born at Santa Clara Pueblo, one of the eight Northern Pueblos in the Rio Grande Valley of Northern New Mexico. Although raised away from the Pueblo, Ms. Reifel has spent much time there. Her goal is to work as a school counselor with Native American children.

Introduction

Non-Native Americans often are admonished to be "sensitive" to cultural differences in interacting with Native Americans. However, the search can range far and wide before finding specific suggestions about *how* to be "sensitive" and to better communicate with them. The usual suggestion for how best to understand Native Americans is to live and work among them for a period of time. However, as Ellis and Anderson (1988) stated, aside from the practical difficulties of gaining experience by "living with them," many workers in the Bureau of Indian Affairs (BIA) attest that mere association is not enough.

Great diversity exists among Native American individuals and tribes, both on and off reservations. Interests, needs, and cultures of Native Americans living on reservations will most likely vary greatly from those of urban Native Americans. Furthermore, differences also are found between Native American groups living in different parts of the United States.

Different cultural groups who have lived many years in the same area may become more alike than cultural groups who have lived far apart for many years. For example, the Pueblo Indians of Northern New Mexico and their Mexican neighbors who arrived there from Mexico hundreds of years ago, have many cultural similarities today. In contrast, a great many cultural differences are in evidence between members of these same Pueblos and members of other Native American nations, i.e., the Navajo and Sioux.

A Brief History of Native Americans

The Native American's role in United States history is long and complex. Unfortunately, this role has been, and continues to be, vastly overlooked by historians. However, Native American culture and history is rich and full, and should be told accurately to all elementary, middle, high school, and college students in America.

Native Americans first met Europeans when Columbus came to "discover" the Americas. From the beginning, Columbus' effect on the Native American was not a positive one. During 1492, Columbus and his followers literally "sold" over 500 Native Americans to Spain as slaves. This practice was officially discontinued in 1500, but slave trade of Native Americans occurred until as late as 1891 (Forbes, 1964). Most Native Americans sold as slaves were used as agricultural labor forces in the Caribbean. However, most United States history texts make little or no mention of Native American slavery.

There were three primary European group influences on Native Americans in the United States: French, Spanish, and English. According to historians, each of these groups treated the Native American differently. The French adopted a "friendly" attitude and desired to co-exist peacefully. The English, on the other hand, were openly hostile to the Native Americans and used brute force against them while the Spanish were somewhere between these two extremes. At first, Spanish missionaries tried to forcibly convert Native Americans to Christianity. Unfortunately, however, the missions in which they lived were more like concentration camps for Native Americans; death rates were extremely high, approximately double the birth rate. Eventually, the Spanish gave up their attempts at conversion of Native Americans in exchange for peaceful relationships with them (Forbes, 1964).

Between the period 1513 and the early twentieth century, the English (i.e., colonial white Americans) fought a relentless series of wars against Native Americans to gain ownership of what is now much of the United States. For example, between 1607 and 1787, American colonists expanded land domination along the Atlantic coast infecting tribe after tribe of Native Americans with disease and instigating warfare along the way, and therefore driving the Native Americans westward (Berkhofer, 1978).

In this time of strife, the "secret weapon" of white American colonists was disease. Measles and small pox wiped out virtually entire tribes of Native Americans. One of the worst diseases given to the Indians was syphilis. Overall, tens of thousands of Native Americans died due to diseases which were unknown among them before the arrival of white colonial Americans (Forbes, 1964).

Of interesting historical significance at this time is the origin of scalping. Contrary to popular opinion, it did not originate with the Native American; it was first used as a method by the English to verify Native American death counts. Thus, it can be assumed that Native Americans adopted "scalping" as a model of European violence, i.e., imitation as an insult to whites, a way to get back at them.

On May 28, 1830, the Indian Removal Act legislation passed the U.S. Congress. It was intended to "remove" all Native Americans east of the Mississippi to the then newly made territory of Oklahoma. Thousands of Native Americans were forced to walk the "Trail of Tears" to reach Oklahoma. Of the 125,000 Native Americans forcibly dislocated, more than 40,000 died. Native Americans were told that Oklahoma was a territory set apart just for them, and that no one could, or ever would, take it from them. Of course, as with many past promises made to Native Americans, this one too was broken.

The utmost faith shall always be observed toward the Indians; their lands and property shall never be taken from them. . . .

(U.S. Congress, 1789)

The Anglo view of Native Americans at that time was that they were "wild savages." They were viewed as stupid and primitive. President Jefferson went so far as to label them "untrainable" (Berkhofer, 1978).

Between 1868 and 1870, the 13th and 14th amendments to the U.S. Constitution were passed. The 13th amendment abolished slavery, but was focused almost exclusively on Blacks even though its provisions were applicable to the Native American. "[N]ative Americans were forced into 'involuntary servitude' by the government on innumerable occasions after 1868, without recourse to judicial procedures" (Forbes, p. 109).

Joe Wittmer, Ph.D.

During the 1870s Native Americans were considered official "wards" of the U.S., and as "wards," they could not become citizens. However, the Constitution does not extend to the government the authority to declare residents "wards" of the U.S.

Forbes (1964) wrote:

It would appear, then, that all of the coercive policies adopted by the federal government from 1870 to 1928 were strictly illegal, since they were in violation of the fourteenth amendment as well as of the first, second, fifth, tenth, and thirteenth amendments. Thus, much of the United States native policy since 1870 has been erected upon a nonexistent legal base (p. 110).

Of particularly great historical significance to Native Americans was the Battle at Wounded Knee which occurred on December 29, 1890. As a reaction to reduction of their reservation lands, the Teton Sioux responded to Wovoka, a Paiute prophet who promised the disappearance of the White man and a return of the buffalo if certain rites and dances were performed. These rites, called the Ghost Dance, caused such an alarm among white Americans that federal military assistance was requested. The military subdued the movement, but several hundred Sioux left their reservation to hide in the Badlands of North Dakota. They were surrounded at Wounded Knee and had nearly been disarmed when a scuffle broke out. A shot was fired killing one of the soldiers. As a result, the soldiers fired rifles and machine guns point blank into the group of Native Americans. More than two hundred Native American men, women, and children, mostly armed with only clubs and knives, were killed in the ensuing riot.

Much later (February 27, 1970), 200 members of the American Indian Movement (AIM) retook Wounded Knee and declared it the "Independent Oglala Sioux Nation." They vowed to stay there until the U.S. met certain demands (e.g., review of all Native American treaties, investigation of Native American treatment, and a change in tribal leaders). Federal marshals surrounded them and the siege ended on May 8, 1970 when the Native Americans surrendered in exchange for promise of negotiations on their grievances.

In 1923, legislation was passed to make all Native American citizens of the U.S. However, it was not totally in effect until 1957. Prior to 1934, the U.S. policy towards Native Americans was to "individualize" them; i.e., to take them off the reservation and

"Americanize" them. In 1934, legislation was passed to halt the destruction of tribal organizations, but it was largely ineffective. What followed were years of relocation policies (Richardson, 1981).

Strongly indicated in American history is that Native Americans have had many reasons to distrust the United States government. And, because of several current positions the government has concerning them, this distrust continues in the 1990s. Torrey (1986) stated that, "Given a century of starvation, struggle, deceit, and disease as white men pursued their 'manifest destiny,' it is no surprise that Native Americans today have little faith in government services" (p. 170).

Most Native Americans simply want to be left alone, to live their way of life without interference. This "leave us alone" concept was best stated several years ago by Alex Chasing Hawk before a Congressional hearing:

> The primary goal and need of Indians today is not for someone to feel sorry for us and claim descent from Pocahontas to make us feel better. Nor do we need to be classified as semi-white and have programs and policies made to bleach us further. Nor do we need further studies to see if we are feasible. We need a new policy by Congress acknowledging our right to live in peace, free from arbitrary harassment. We need the public at large to drop the myths in which it has clothed us for so long. We need fewer and fewer "experts" on Indians.

> What we need is a cultural leave-us-alone agreement, in spirit and in fact (cited in Deloria, 1973, p. 50).

One final note in this brief section on history concerns the Religious Freedom Act of 1975. For Native Americans, this legislation allowed the continuing practice of their religion as done for hundreds of years. Unfortunately, this act was rescinded in 1990! The official reason was that certain Native American rites included the use of peyote, a hallucinogen. The use of this product is illegal, and therefore the religious rite is now illegal.

Demographics

It has been estimated that when Columbus arrived in the Americas, there were more than one million Native Americans in the land that later became America. By 1850 this population had been reduced to approximately 250,000 individuals. The largest current Native American populations exist in California, Oklahoma, Arizona, and New Mexico. The Navajos are the largest tribe at more than 146,000 people (USA Today, 1991), and America's Native American population is growing at a rapid pace.

Poverty and alcoholism are two of the greatest problems facing Native Americans today. Of the various racial groups in the United States, Native Americans are the poorest, have the worst living conditions, and the worst health. Twenty-eight percent of Native Americans live on income below the poverty level, compared to 12.4% for all other races in the United States. Their average income is less than $16,000, compared to $23,100 for all other racially defined groups. And, the outlook remains bleak, e.g., among the Navajo, the unemployment rate is 33.9%; half of the population (75,000) has no electricity and 55% of their homes lack running water (USA Today, 1991).

Sue and Sue (1990) presented the following data: One out of three Native Americans will be jailed in his or her lifetime; every other Native American family will have a relative die in jail; between 25% and 35% of Native American children are separated from their families and placed in foster homes, adoptive homes, or institutions; and between 40% and 80% of tribal members are unemployed.

According to government figures recorded by the U.S. Census Bureau in 1980, there were 1,418,195 Native Americans residing in North America. About 700,000 live on reservations today. The rest are "card carrying Indians," so-called because of the Bureau of Indian Affairs (BIA) cards issued to Native Americans who receive government allotments or assistance of any kind.

Some Common Characteristics of Native Americans

There are many characteristics that can be readily attributed to Native Americans. However, it is again important to note that each of these characteristics must be *considered individually*, rather than *expected* for a group or members of a specific tribe.

Several writers have identified some value related characteristics common to many Native Americans:

1. They place high value on behavior that is harmonious to all, and on behavior that does not call attention to the individual. Behavior which calls attention to self is considered egotistical, and goes against one of the most important Native American values (Dillard, 1983).

2. Native Americans may appear to be agreeing with what you are saying, but then not follow through with the behavior expected. Unfortunately, throughout history, this type of behavior has lead Anglo Americans to believe that Native Americans are dishonest and untrustworthy. However, this is simply an extension of the principle in which the individual does not want to go "against the grain." The Native American culture does not approve of dishonesty, contrary to existing myth or stereotype. However, Native Americans have been known to go to great lengths to develop misdirection and ambiguities to avoid disagreement or contradiction with others. In the American majority point of view, such behavior is synonymous with telling untruths because it does not clarify the truth. However, of more value to Native Americans is the fact that contradiction and disagreement are disharmonious and are to be avoided whenever possible. Furthermore, to disagree with someone is in one sense an assertion of ego and individuality. Therefore, Native Americans work hard at appearing to be in agreement (Anderson & Ellis, 1988).

3. Traditional Native Americans place high value on the opinions and attitudes of tribal brothers and sisters. They are very sensitive to opinions of peers (Dillard, 1983).

Joe Wittmer, Ph.D.

4. Traditional Native Americans live in the "here and now," and are not enthusiastic about setting long term goals such as furthering education or extending a career. Again, these actions or behaviors contrary to this may be viewed as egotistical or self-centered.

5. There is little regard among Native Americans for what is considered "personal wealth." Any gain is to be for the tribe or family, rather than for the individual. Variation from this perspective is seen as selfish. Richardson (1981), a Native American, wrote that he had never known a wealthy Indian. He also related an incident when a Native American, having just received a large allotment of money, spent all of it on a large truck filled with beer and then shared it with the entire tribe at a big party. Richardson indicated that most Anglos would find this lacking in logic and common sense, and being irresponsible. But, that is where the Native American and Anglo values differ greatly—to the Indian, buying the truck load of beer represented fun and happiness and a way to share with the entire tribe.

6. There is tribal influence among Native Americans for valuing personal strength, embracing self control, intelligence and wisdom.

7. Native Americans emphasize obedience to the law, unselfishness, responsibility, kindness, and cooperation. However, respect must be earned.

8. Composure, good judgment, and tranquility are valued among Native Americans.

9. Peaceful and nonaggressive behaviors are emphasized by Native Americans. Shy, unassertive, and passive behavior is the norm (Dillard, 1983).

10. Many Native Americans believe in the concept of "oneness with the universe." Preservation of all living species, both plant and animal, is paramount.

11. Native Americans hold great respect for their elders; they are viewed as valued teachers.

12. The manner in which Native Americans experience time is a part of their relationship with nature and the universe; it is a religious type of relationship they have with their world (Dillard, 1983).

Understanding the concept of time among Native Americans is particularly important in communication with them. If you have a Native American friend and your relationship involves coordinating events or scheduled activities, you may have to make some major adjustments to accommodate the Native American sense of time. A chronological, linear sense of time is the most widely shared characteristic of American and European cultures. However, Native American cultures share a *ceremonial* time sense. Native American writer Paula Gunn Allen (1986), in her book *The Sacred Hoop,* clearly delineated the differences of the "in time sense" between the two cultures:

> Chronological time structure is useful in promoting and supporting an industrial time sense. The idea that everything has a starting point and an ending point reflects accurately the process by which industry produces goods. Western industrialists engage in time-motion studies hoping to enhance profits. Chronological organization also supports allied Western beliefs that the individual is separate from the environment, that man is separate from God, that life is an isolated business, and that the person who controls the events around him is a hero.... This contrasts sharply with a ceremonial time sense that assumes the individual as a moving event shaped by and shaping human and nonhuman surroundings....
>
> Ultimately, Indian time is a concept based on a sense of propriety, on a ritual understanding of order and harmony. For an Indian, if being on time means being out of harmony with self and ritual, the Indian will be 'late.' The right time for a tribal Indian is the time when he or she is in balance with the flow of the four rivers (p. 149).

Sue and Sue (1990) wrote that Native Americans value being in the present. Thus, "rushing them" is viewed as lack of respect. A problem in communication may result since both parties may sense things are not going well; for one it is too slow and for the other too fast. Sue and Sue also suggested that Native Americans, because of their present-time orientation, are more likely to expect immediate, concrete solutions as opposed to future-oriented "abstract goals." The latter may explain some of the problems Native Americans have with the "slow" future-oriented solutions of the American government on their behalf.

Traditional Native Americans' apparent disregard for time (structure) has given rise to the stereotype of their being shiftless, lazy, and undependable. However, time measurement is a fairly recent innovation in western civilization and is necessary only in a culture that values change; i.e., the American-Anglo culture. Change exists only within the context of time and for a culture that values stability and actively discourages change, time is an unimportant consideration. Little support exists among many Native Americans for future plans because such plans imply that the individual is trying to better himself or herself at the expense of the tribe (Anderson & Ellis, 1988). Those who value "doing things on schedule" might have problems communicating with those who value integrated, ceremonial time. Once more, it is important to stress that characteristics are often tribal specific, as well as specific to individuals, and are not necessarily representative of all Native Americans.

Some Modern Concerns

Since the white man's arrival on this continent nearly five hundred years ago, much destruction of the Native Americans' culture and religions has occurred. Seemingly, the assimilation of Native Americans into the dominant culture has been the goal. While other minority groups have struggled to be accepted into the dominant culture, many Native Americans have undergone *unwanted* assimilation (Richardson, 1981).

One method of "forced" assimilation was through imposition of Christianity on Native Americans. And, there has been a wide range of acceptance of Christianity among Native Americans. For example, some Pueblos have been Catholics for many generations, but also continue their tribal religious activities. However, many "traditional" Native Americans do not view Christianity as good for them, and, in actuality, view it as a detriment to their way of life.

Many pressures are forcing Native Americans to leave the reservation. According to Anderson and Ellis (1988), the primary causes are public school systems with the value systems inherent in them, and television, with its fantasy-consumption value system.

Non-Native Americans may have difficulty appreciating the trauma of Native Americans who leave reservations. The trauma results when they must leave behind a value system that has provided nurturance for all of their lives and suddenly being forced to adopt a system of being independent and alone for which they have neither preparation nor relevant role-models. This can be traumatic and often causes psychological conflicts (Anderson & Ellis, 1988).

Even for those who do not leave their tribal home, changes promoted by the U.S. Government have eroded some traditional ways of life, e.g., the Eisenhower administration provided social services only to those who left the reservation. In the 1970s, the U.S. Department of Housing and Urban Development (HUD) offered a newly constructed, "modern" house to each Pueblo Indian who headed a household. Before that, almost all of the Pueblo housing had been constructed the traditional way; a married daughter built rooms attached to her mother's house and she and her husband remained there to raise their family. HUD's offer of new houses did not recognize this tradition and actually eroded it by bringing about the building of new single-family houses on separate pieces of land. Sadly, modern Pueblo housing now looks very much like suburban America.

Because dominant cultures set the standards of what is "normal" for American society, Native Americans and other minorities who hold different value systems are frequently the victims of prejudice. The "cowboy" movies have not helped—the "good guys" always wear white hats while the "bad guys" wear feathered headbands! The burden of adapting to (or at least giving the appearance of adapting to) Anglo values, culture, and religion has been forced on Native Americans. Little effort has been made to better understand Native Americans or for more effective communication with them.

Fortunately, there have always been those non-Native Americans who value cultural pluralism. If not for people valuing cultural pluralism, Native Americans would most likely have been totally assimilated long ago. Cultural pluralists have sought to understand the worldviews and specific cultures of Native Americans as well as to facilitate understanding and communication among cultures.

Nature and Religion

O our Mother the Earth, O our Father the Sky...
Weave for us a garment of brightness;
May the warp be the white light of morning,
May the weft be the red light of evening,
May the fringes be the falling rain,
May the border be the standing rainbow.
Thus weave for us a garment of brightness,
That we may walk fittingly where birds sing,
That we may walk fittingly where grass is green,
O our Mother the Earth, O our Father the Sky.

(Song of the Sky Loom—Tewa)

The above song illustrates how traditional Native Americans feel about the Earth and nature in general. The Earth is their Mother and plays a major role in their religious beliefs. Religion, in traditional Native American cultures, is not a separate part of life to be celebrated one day a week; it is a part of daily life. It is a minute-by-minute celebration of everyday existence. It is an awareness of how a Native American is connected to all of creation through transformation of the cycles of the Earth.

It has been the land that has held the tribe together as a people, through generations of shared experiences. It is knowing that the layers of Earth on which they live is literally the bodies of their people who, in death, continue to provide sustenance for man and growing plants and animals. Plants, animals, and man are all brothers and sisters in a biological sense, transformed by cycles of creation. Richardson (1981), a Native American writer, stated; "Native people cannot conceive of a zoo that pens up their 'brothers and sisters,' the four-legged, the two-legged, and the creatures that crawl. They feel that all that walk, fly and swim must live in harmony with one another—it is God's wish." (p. 242)

Writers often interpret Native American religions as mystical or animistic. Traditional Native Americans take care of Mother Earth since the earth is their home forever. They are not going to leave earth one day for "a better place;" they take care not to damage the environment, their home! Many feel this is a lesson they have to offer Christians. As a Native American friend stated, "How much loyalty can you have for a place if you plan to someday leave it?" To most Americans, land has commercial, agricultural, or aesthetic value, but to Native Americans, the land is sacred.

One does not sell the earth upon which the people walk.

(Crazy Horse—Sioux)

This attitude regarding the Earth is deeply ingrained as Native Americans do not talk casually about buying and selling land. To do so is equivalent to saying that you are planning to transfer title to your parents to a stranger. The concept is natural to Native Americans, but is often misunderstood by others.

Joe Wittmer, Ph.D.

Nonverbal Communication

Nonverbal communication is important in establishing a relationship with Native Americans. If one is moving too fast physically, or relating using body language that appears threatening, then relationships with Native Americans may not progress past mere introduction. Some of the areas about which to be sensitive are eye contact, distance between persons during communication, touching, and hurrying interactions, i.e., wanting to get right down to business rather than establishing rapport and trust through an extended general conversation.

In mainstream American culture, emphasis is placed on maintaining eye contact during communication. However, traditional Native Americans rarely look another person in the eye when conversing. They will look off into the distance, down at the ground, and over the head of the person to whom they are speaking. The power of eye contact and of human vision is highly respected, and therefore used rarely and cautiously among Native Americans.

Many Native Americans prefer to maintain some distance from another person when talking. When greeting a Native American, a simple nod of the head may be better than a handshake. Or, a gentle clasping of the hand may be more appropriate than a vigorous handshake. A basic approach is to try and follow the lead of the individual with whom you are conversing. They will show you what they are most comfortable with as a greeting and/or speaking distance.

Some Recommendations

Sue and Sue (1990), writing to counselors and psychologists, stated:

> Before working with American Indians, it is important to be aware of your own cultural biases. Much of what we do is based on Western values and influences. We expect clients to establish good eye contact, to discuss inner feeling, and to verbalize concerns. American Indians often will not display these behaviors. In working with adolescents, we often work toward having them develop increasing independence from their parents. We also see the nuclear family as the basic unit. For American Indians, interdependence with the extended family might be the goal. As parents, they are often much more permissive in their childrearing practices. It is important to be aware of how cultural influences have shaped our perception of ideal situations. It is also important to avoid stereotypes of what an individual Indian is like. Instead, it is critical to respond to the individual and identify and explore his or her values (p. 186).

It is my opinion that the above statement by Sue and Sue can be directly applied to increasing positive interpersonal communication with Native Americans.

Anderson and Ellis (1988) listed the following preparatory steps as very important for anyone working with Native Americans and/or hoping to communicate more effectively with members of this group:

1. Recognize that Native Americans may approach life with different expectations, values, and interpretations of events than you do. Also, recognize that their approach to life is as satisfying and rich to them as any other style of life is to other people.

2. Become familiar with specific Native American cultural values so as to better understand and appreciate the pressures being faced by Native Americans.

3. Resist the temptation to interpret a specific behavior or problem as if it emerged in a manner typical of that problem in a non-Native American society. That is, do not interpret their behavior in terms of your specific culture.

Joe Wittmer, Ph.D.

4. Appreciate that Native Americans, like everyone else, want minimal stress and aggravation in their lives.

5. Converse with Native Americans with an attitude of sincere respect (rather than of paternalism or sympathy).

According to Sue and Sue (1990), Native Americans place high value on the spiritual quality of being. Value is placed on the attainment of inner fulfillment. And, since every person is fulfilling a purpose, Native Americans believe that no one should have the power to impose values on another human being (Sue and Sue, 1990). Thus, untimely advice or evaluation may greatly impede communication with a Native American. Richardson (1981), a Native American, also indicated that when communicating with a Native American, minimize your authority role and be cautious about giving *any* advice. Richardson (1981) further indicated that, when meeting Native Americans for the first time, begin with a soft voice. And, if you must stare, he suggested that you focus your gaze at the floor and listen. Richardson stated that Native Americans are humble people. Thus, when shaking hands, as noted, do so softly. According to Richardson (1981) it is typical of humble people to shake hands in this manner.

Richardson (1981) also suggests the following for improving communication: admit your ignorance, look for and see the positives in Native American culture, listen carefully and do not talk too much. Be realistic and accepting, do not lecture them under any circumstances, always show honor and respect, do not analyze their actions, and, do not under any circumstances, be condescending or deceptive.

Specific customs are important to members of any Indian Nation. It is easy to offend others if you do not know their customs. It is usually helpful first to explain who *you* are, where you are from, and to speak about things in general before asking a Native American for information about himself or herself. Also, try to ask questions in a gentle manner and pay special attention to the answers received. It also would be good to learn how the Native American to whom you are talking refers to his or her people, home, ancestral village, and tribal heritage. Even words such as "tribe" or "reservation" may not be understood by some Native Americans. They may live in a pueblo (village) and may, for example, refer to their people by the name of the specific pueblo. Or, you may be speaking to a Navajo, who is part of the Navajo Nation and knows little of the pueblo. Ask gently for knowledge and information that leads to better understanding.

If you will be working closely with Native Americans, try to gain information about their religious affiliation (if any), the holidays they celebrate (traditional and "regular") and the form of the celebration, and perhaps some history of their village, band, tribe, or nation. These are very important aspects of Native American culture. Libraries can be particularly helpful for finding this type of information.

If you are invited into a Native American home, you will, most likely, be treated as an honored quest. If you are offered something to eat or drink, it would be considered rude to refuse. The foods you would be served may be quite different from what you are used to, but may be considered honored foods among the people whom you are visiting.

Finally, in facilitating interpersonal communication with Native Americans, the first and most important thing to do is to become aware of how you have been "shaped" and defined by your own culture, and how this shaping has contributed to the cultural expectations and norms by which you judge others. It also is important to understand your own worldview and how it is shared by members of your own culture. Only by fully understanding, and being able to articulate your own worldview, will you be able to understand and share in the culture and perceptions of Native Americans.

Summary

Native Americans have often been portrayed as savage and uncivilized and were viewed as a nuisance by the expansionist mentality of America's Anglo forefathers. They were seen as people who were better off dead, locked up, or set aside on a reservation somewhere out of sight. In actuality, Native American civilizations were highly ordered, closely integrated societies that lived in relative harmony with their environment. They took and used only what they needed for survival. To them, nature was their God and was treated with utmost respect, unlike most Anglos who made nature a servant to be used solely for man's purposes.

Native Americans find it difficult to trust their "white brothers," and positive communication between the two is sometimes difficult. However, effective communication is possible if we simply become aware of, and sensitive to, our similarities and differences.

References

Allen, P.G. (1986). *The sacred hoop.* New York, NY: Beacon Press.

Anderson, J. M., & Ellis, R., "On the reservation," in Vacc, N. A., Wittmer, J. & DeVaney, S. B. (eds.) pp. 107-126 (1988). *Experiencing and counseling multicultural and diverse populations.* Muncie, IN: Accelerated Development.

Berkhofer, R.F. (1978). *The white man's Indian: Images of the American Indian from Columbus to the present.* New York, NY: Knopf.

Deloria, V. (1973). *God is red.* New York: Dell Publishing.

Dillard, J. M. (1983). *Multicultural counseling: Toward ethnic and cultural relevance in human encounters.* Chicago, IL: Nelson-Hall.

Forbes, J.D. (1964). *The Indian in America's past.* Englewood Cliffs, NJ: Prentice-Hall.

Richardson, E.R. (1981). "Cultural and historical perspectives in counseling American Indians." In Sue, D., (ed.) *Counseling the culturally different: Theory and practice,* pp. 216-255 New York: Wiley.

Sue, D., & Sue, D. (1990). *Counseling the culturally different: Theory and practice.* New York: Wiley.

Torrey, E. (1986). *Witchdoctors and psychiatrists.* Northvale, NJ: Jason Aronson.

USA Today (5/9/91). "Life on the reservation."

Questions for
Discussion and Reflection

1. What stereotypes do people still hold concerning Native Americans? Create a list of ten such stereotypes and briefly indicate the "reason" or "roots" of each (in your opinion). How might each of these affect communication?

2. How might certain cultural values held by Native Americans be exploited by the majority culture? Select three such values and explain how this might occur.

3. Which Native American characteristics given in this chapter contrast the most with your own? Would these differences affect communication between you? How?

4. Assume the role of a Native American and write a short essay titled, *"How the West Was Won."*

Section III

The Facilitative Model of Communication

Chapter IX

Characteristics of Facilitative Communicators

Chapter X

Verbal Responses: From Least to Most Facilitative

Chapter XI

Using the Facilitative Responses: A Summary

The Facilitative Model was first developed and published by Joe Wittmer and Robert D. Myrick in 1974 in a book titled, *Facilitative Teaching: Theory and Practice* (Santa Monica, CA: Goodyear Publishing Company). The Facilitative Model has also appeared, in one form or another, in the following books:

Myrick, R.D., & Erney, T. (1978). *Caring and Sharing: Becoming a Peer Facilitator.* Minneapolis, MN: Educational Media Corporation.

Myrick, R.D., & Erney, T. (1979). *Youth Helping Youth: A Handbook for Training Peer Facilitators.* Minneapolis MN: Educational Media Corporation.

Wittmer, J., & Myrick, R.D. (1980). *Facilitative Teaching: Theory and Practice* (a revision). Minneapolis, MN: Educational Media Corporation.

Myrick, R.D., & Bowman, R.P. (1981a). *Becoming a Friendly Helper.* Minneapolis, MN: Educational Media Corporation.

Myrick, R.D., & Bowman, R.P. (1981b). *Children Helping Children.* Minneapolis, MN: Educational Media Corporation.

Myrick, R.D. & Sorenson, D.L. (1988). *Peer Helping: A Practical Guide.* Minneapolis, MN. Educational Media Corporation.

Wittmer, J. & Myrick, R.D. (1989). *The Teacher as Facilitator.* Minneapolis, MN. Educational Media Corporation.

Myrick, R.D. (1987). *Developmental Guidance and Counseling: A Practical Approach.* Minneapolis, MN. Educational Media Corporation.

Myrick, R.D., & Folk, B.E. (1991). *Peervention: Training Peer Facilitators for Prevention Education.* Minneapolis, MN. Educational Media Corporation.

As the above book titles indicate, the Facilitative Model has been applied to teaching, school counseling, and peer facilitation in the schools. However, in the chapters that follow, I have attempted to apply the model to *interpersonal* communication. I am not aware of any particular communication theory or model that specifically addresses multicultural communication. And, it is not my intent to imply that the facilitative communication model presented here will apply to all cultural groups in America. In addition, it should be acknowledged that not everyone, regardless of cultural background, will find the model and skills presented to fit their needs, personality, and so forth. However, I do believe that using the facilitative responses presented (in an appropriate and timely manner) herein will assist in bridging the communication gap in your personal relationships with others regardless of culture, race, gender, or religion.

No attempt has been made to specifically reference the above publications. However, I hereby acknowledge their contributions to this book and appreciation is extended to the writers and the publishers for their contributions.

Chapter *IX*

Characteristics of Facilitative Communicators

How can facilitative communicators be identified? Many people demonstrate one or more of the characteristics of such people, and they are usually recognized by their peers and friends as "really helpful" or "easy to talk to." However, it is more difficult to find individuals who exhibit all the important characteristics; people usually described as "caring, kind, wonderful, thoughtful, interested, and sensitive." Where they are found, healthy, meaningful relationships flourish from their communication patterns, regardless of their or another's race, religion, culture, and so forth.

One day we will learn that the heart can never be totally right if the head is totally wrong. Only through the bringing together of head and heart—intelligence and goodness—shall man rise to a fulfillment of his true nature.

Dr. Martin Luther King

Although there are others, I begin here with several characteristics which identify those who are fully effective, facilitative communicators; people who communicate well with those similar and those different, are:

1. attentive listeners,

2. genuine/authentic,

3. accepting/trustworthy,

4. understanding, and

5. respectful.

In addition, culturally skilled communicators are:

6. knowledgeable of other cultures,

7. aware of their own assumptions, cultural values, and biases, and

8. value the learning and using of facilitative communication skills.

The latter implies that they are willing to spend the necessary time needed to acquire more effective interpersonal communication skills (these skills are the focus of Chapter Ten). Let us look at these eight characteristics in more detail.

Facilitative Communicators are Attentive Listeners

Problems in communication often result from poor listening skills. Although it seems like a simple thing to do, and we often take it for granted, attentive listening requires both effort and skill. When people feel understood, it is both a satisfying and an exciting experience for them. This is usually true regardless of their cultural backgrounds. When people feel that they have been heard, there is a reduction in the psychological distance that usually exists between talkers and listeners.

The four Chinese characters that make up the verb "to listen" are: ear, eyes, undivided attention and heart.

Joe Wittmer, Ph.D.

Most people do not encounter many effective listeners. In fact, many counselors and psychotherapists make their living simply by being good listeners. How often do you feel people really listen to you? How do you know if they have really heard you?

The next time you are with a group of people, note how well each person listens and responds to you and the others. Unless it is an unusual group, the conversation typically will jump from one person to another, with little real (i.e., two-way) communication going on. For example, one person might begin by expressing concern about our country's inability to find a cure for cancer. The usual response is to relate that particular idea to the listener's experiences, without responding directly. For example, "You know I've been thinking of the same thing. I read something similar the other day and thought...." At this point the focus moves to a new talker, while the first talker can only guess if his or her message was ever received.

In everyday talking/listening practices, many times people are simply waiting for a speaker to stop talking so they can say something. Listeners often only hear the first few words spoken, and then their minds rush quickly ahead to what *they* want to say. Often, the listener's silence, while waiting a turn to speak, represents a period of tolerance more than a period of listening.

Picture yourself in a group. How many times have you tuned in and out of a discussion? What do you do as the conversation drifts from person to person? Is the conversation really only a collection of unrelated sounds and visual impressions?

One often hears the remark "He talks too much," but when did anyone last hear the criticism "He listens too much?"

Norman R. Augustine

Listening is highly affected by our motivations and feelings. And while they may not be the same across all cultures, they do change, which makes listening a shifting process regardless of the speaker.

Effective listeners want to know what another person is thinking and feeling, which has a powerful influence on listening behavior. When we are unable to keep our focus on someone, we may react to our "hidden" feelings or motives, and therefore

---

reject the ideas or feelings the other person is attempting to communicate. In such instances we become poor listeners. It is likely that many communication problems are caused by inattention and unmotivated listening. What determines whether you attend to something being said? Does race or cultural background play a role in how well you attend? Hopefully not.

When listening to a person, we tend to select that which is most pertinent to us. We learn to be "selective" listeners because of the tendencies both to enhance ourselves and to find some way in which we identify with the speaker. We seldom tolerate ambiguity or incongruence.

We do not have to be ineffective listeners. For example, we might be sitting in a restaurant and trying to enjoy dinner and conversation with friends. An objective analysis of sounds in the room would indicate a clutter of noise, sounds from the kitchen, scuffling feet, clanging glasses, and other people talking around us. Yet, if we are really interested in what a friend is saying, we will pay close attention and hear that person. We will focus on that person's words with "vacuum sweeper" listening. We will close out the distractions around us, unless someone brings into our awareness a particularly distracting sound or our attention wanes.

The Telephone

I have just hung up; why did he telephone?
I don't know.... Oh! I get it....
I talked a lot and listened very little.
Forgive me, Lord, it was a monologue
and not a dialogue.

I explained my idea and did not get his;
Since I didn't listen, I learned nothing;
Since I didn't listen, I didn't help.
Since I didn't listen, we didn't commune.

Forgive me, Lord, for we were connected,
And now we are cut off.

Michael Quoist

Joe Wittmer, Ph.D.

Attending is the process of acknowledging particular stimuli from an environment. Thus, listening is a selective attending process in which we choose to hear those things that most fit our needs, purposes, and desires. Sometimes we select a stimulus because of its suddenness, intensity, or contrast to what we have been experiencing. Other times, there are sounds, i.e., stimuli, that we tend to hear because of habit. Sometimes we listen and focus upon things to which we have learned to attend.

In *The Miracle of The Dialogue,* Revel Howe cited the case of the Baptist who was overheard saying to the Episcopalian, "I cannot hear you because of what I expect you to say." How often does what we expect (maybe a bias or a stereotype) someone to say get in the way of our hearing what that person is actually saying?

If a listener expects a prejudicial response, for example, there is a high probability that whenever the talker speaks the listener will perceive that person as being prejudiced. The effects of such mind sets are significant, especially in intercultural communications. Expectations often are detrimental to effective listening. We are not always aware of our mind sets, and even if we are, they are difficult to control. Therefore, it is important that we develop habits that help us go beyond what we expect in a situation.

Most of us do not think of ourselves as being prejudiced. But, prejudice plays a big part in most of our efforts to communicate. These are not necessarily strong, overt kinds of prejudice, but rather subtle, hidden ones. We have blind spots about ourselves and these effect our listening habits.

Perhaps the prejudice which proves most damaging of all is the assumption that we know what another person is going to say before that person says it, or that we fully understand what is meant while it is being said. The truth may be that we have only accepted the words on the surface. We think we know the person speaking, and we allow ourselves to hear that which verifies or agrees with what we think we know about the person. This kind of thinking becomes a vicious circle. The person continues to speak, and we may erroneously go on assuring that person that we know what was meant, when in fact we do not know or understand.

Success comes from listening. I've never learned anything by talking.

Lou Holtz

Effective listening also involves hearing "deeper" levels of communication. That is, a good listener attends to literal meanings, but also makes a special effort to understand the more personal meanings of the speaker's words. The good listener tunes in on the feelings and attitudes that underlie the topic or the literal words. The listener who wants to become an effective communicator hears the words, but responds to both the ideas and the feelings underlying them. There is an awareness of the personal meanings that accompany spoken words.

Guidelines for Effective Listening

Many people have suggested guidelines for improving listening habits. Following are among the most common:

1. **Look directly at the person speaking.** Although some cultures place more emphasis on eye contact than do others, eye contact, even if fleeting, communicates that you are attending to what is being said.

2. **Avoid being preoccupied with your own thoughts.** Do not rush ahead with your own ideas; rather, give attention to the way things are being said, the tone of the voice, the particular words or expressions being used, and bodily gestures that all are parts of the communication process.

3. **Try to listen for more than just spoken words.** A speaker's feelings and attitudes are also communicated in what is being said.

4. **Say something to the speaker which communicates that you are following the conversation.** Keep the speaker talking. Be an active listener.

5. **Do not evaluate or judge others.** Listening in a nonjudgmental way will help you stay open and make you more sensitive to the person, their cultural values, ideas, and so forth.

Joe Wittmer, Ph.D.

When we speak we do not listen, my son and I. I complain of slights, hurts inflicted on me. He sings a counterpoint, but not in harmony. Asking a question, he doesn't wait to hear. Trying to answer, I interrupt his refrain. This comic opera excels in disharmony only.

Lenni Goldstein

Listening is perhaps the most important characteristic in facilitating communication with others. A good listener communicates both interest and respect. Listening seems like a simple thing to do, but often it is difficult to put into practice. As noted, for most people, listening is simply waiting a turn to talk, almost a common courtesy. This is not what is meant here by effective, facilitative communication that involves good listening. If you are a good listener, you avoid breaking in to direct the conversation or make remarks that take the focus away from the person who is talking. And, you work at avoiding being preoccupied with your own thoughts. You do not let your mind wander or anticipate what the person is going to say.

Good listening, however, is not a passive activity; it is not just waiting or sitting back until the person has finished talking. Rather, good listening is an active process where we communicate that we are striving to understand what the person is saying; we say something to show that we heard!

We restrict some of our remarks in order to give others an opportunity to talk and we let them tell their stories in their own ways, but we also participate in the conversation. A primary distinction is that good listeners "follow the lead" of another's conversation, i.e., stay with that person's thoughts, ideas, and feelings, rather than initiating new directions.

Following the lead of the talker requires both patience and practice. The skills used involve listening to the words being said and focusing on *everything* the person is communicating, including nonverbal communications. This means using not only your ears, but also your eyes (or other sense receptors, such as touch, if appropriate). Good listeners constantly ask themselves, "What is the message here? What is this person really saying? What is going on in this person right now?"

Listening is essential (almost) no matter the task. It may be simply gaining information, having a casual talk, or encouraging a person to talk in depth about personal experiences. "Everybody's talkin' at me," sings the vagabond youth in the novel and motion picture, *Midnight Cowboy*. This could be anybody's song. Most people talk far more than they listen. Even when they give the appearance of listening, most are not really hearing (all of) what is being said. Listening is not easy; most of us have to work hard to do it right.

Facilitative Communicators are Genuine

Regardless of suggestions or guidelines offered for listening, and of any models or patterns of communication, effective listening inevitably depends upon a person's genuine interest. Are you *genuinely* concerned about how another thinks and feels? For example, do you *genuinely* care to know about the experiences of someone culturally different from you? Do you *genuinely* want greater understanding of the attitudes and values that influence the speaker? Are you *genuinely* interested in knowing what makes the person tick? Are you *genuinely* willing to accept another's worldview without evaluation? Are you *genuinely* willing to give the person the "benefit of the doubt?"

"Telling it like it is" has become a popular expression. People are suspicious of others who talk one way and live another. People deplore hypocrisy. It is a time for truthful, caring, honest, and genuine communication. Genuineness implies authenticity. It denotes being in tune with yourself and acting in ways that reveal self-congruence. It means *not* playing a role. It is extremely difficult to feel one thing and communicate another; the truth will win out. For example, if you are prejudiced and have a habit of patronizing others, rest assured they will know it! They may not verbally communicate this to you, but they are aware of such attitudes. And, as Littlejohn and Henderson stated (Chapter 5), minority group individuals are wary of dominate cultural members who are not sincere in their communicative interaction. They further stated that "genuineness" is the characteristic that must be present if communication with African Americans is to be effective. All people, regardless of culture, "see through" phony people.

Effective communicators also avoid playing a role as a facilitative communicator. They avoid thinking: "it is time to play facilitator again." If the facilitative communication process is not genuine, it confuses the person being talked to, and eventually makes the other person suspicious. Of course, such suspicion creates defensiveness. Being "phony" in a relationship also may be harmful. As noted, feeling one thing and communicating another is *not* facilitative, and is easily recognized by the communicatee.

Even genuineness by itself (i.e., without use of other facilitative skills) can be facilitative. It sometimes makes unknowing facilitative communicators of persons simply because others can depend upon them for an honest response. Some persons, even though they have worked hard, studied, and practiced under the best instructors, still will not be as facilitative as others because they "play" at being facilitative communicators.

Whatever the word 'truth' may mean in other spheres, in the realm between man and man it means that one can impart oneself to the other as what one is.... It is a question of the authenticity of what is between men, and without which there can be no authentic human existence. It is no easy thing to be confirmed by the other in one's essence. Therefore, one looks to appearance for aid. To give in to this tendency is the real cowardice of man; to withstand it is his real courage.

Martin Buber

When you assume a role not characteristic of yourself, your ability to communicate effectively with others decreases, especially with culturally different persons.

Keep in mind, as you continue reading this section, that there will be times when you feel awkward and uncomfortable attempting to be a facilitative communicator, and you will wonder whether you are being phony; whether you need more time and practice. People often, and naturally so, feel awkward trying out new behaviors. With practice you *can* learn to integrate the communication skills presented in the next chapter into your own personality; and you will feel more genuine and spontaneous as time goes on.

Being genuine with another implies direct personal encounter, meeting on a person to person basis without defensiveness on the part of either. There is no attempt to retreat to a facade or role. If we do not understand something about another's culture, for example, and how it relates to our current conversation, we simply ask the person, genuinely, for clarification. Thus, genuineness is in a sense being open and honest to one's own experiences. The facilitative communicator realizes that genuineness is the key to "recovering," i.e., correcting for those times when you know you have goofed, especially when talking with someone different from you. To recover, you talk about things honestly, and, as mentioned by several contributors in Section Two of this book, simply ask for clarification from the speaker.

As noted above, there is no real alternative to genuineness in communicating with others. Even if a person is shrewd, it is doubtful the person can hide real feelings from others. When people pretend to care, or to respect, or to be open, they fool only themselves—especially in cross-cultural communication.

As noted above, there *will* be times when you may not feel completely genuine. You may even feel as if you are playing a role when practicing some of the skills in this book. However, if you continue to practice these new skills, they become a part of your normal way of "genuinely" responding to others. And, you will find yourself becoming spontaneous in using them!

Joe Wittmer, Ph.D.

Facilitative Communicators are Accepting and Trustworthy

It is difficult, if not impossible, to accept and respect ourselves if we are not accepted and respected by others. Therefore, one of the important principles of communicating facilitatively with others, regardless of race or cultural background, is acceptance. Acceptance means having empathy (which is very different from sympathy) and recognizing that the person is a unique individual and worthy of respect regardless of race, creed, or religion. *All* individuals are worthy.

If we are to enhance others' self-concepts, and effective facilitative communicators do, then we want to create situations in which others feel relatively free from threat—a trusting relationship. Threat narrows and restricts human behavior and makes solution of problems much more difficult. If, as a facilitator, you are accepting and nonjudgmental, then a trusting, nonthreatening communication environment is created. Ideas and feelings can be explored in more detail. The more we feel we are understood and accepted by others, the more likely we will take risks in the exploration process, and grow as human beings.

Listening and understanding are important characteristics, but in and of themselves they are not enough. They must be combined with a genuine acceptance, trust, and respect, and, as mentioned previously, if the person is a member of a different culture, *knowledge* of that culture. This is not always easy to do, and is particularly difficult when we see others as being different from ourselves. Experts indicate that we have a "natural tendency" to ignore or reject those who are different from us. If this difference is threatening to our own self-concepts, we become critical, sometimes even belittling or condemning, biased, and prejudiced, i.e., the KKK. Our own needs for self-esteem and security may interfere with our accepting and respecting others. Therefore, the more secure of our sense of self, the more we are able to be accepting and trustworthy. Acceptance leads to understanding, and most of us want to be understood, regardless of our cultural heritage or background.

It is important to emphasize that accepting others does not mean that we must *condone* or agree with their thoughts, ideas, and behaviors. Accepting people recognize that others are unique and are doing the best they can to satisfy their needs and to get along in "their" worlds. Accepting does not mean that we necessarily encourage others to continue to do what they are doing. It implies that we accept their feelings and them as "people," but not necessarily that we agree with their behaviors. This is an important distinction in the facilitative model of communication. We recognize that they must assume responsibility for their actions as well as for changes that may occur because of our communication with them.

Facilitative Communicators Show Empathic Understanding

Although being genuine, accepting, and trustworthy are all important in communicating with others, this does not mean necessarily that a person understands another. As we listen genuinely and discover another's perceptions and cultural "worldview," we begin to understand the person. Following this, we can be more genuine and accepting because we can then also be more empathic. We can "tune in" with empathy, the "third ear" of listening.

Empathy means fully understanding other persons, at both cognitive levels, i.e. their cultural values, ways, and so forth, and emotional levels, i.e. their thoughts, ideas, and feelings. Empathy involves going beyond the mere words and intellectual ideas to deeper levels of understanding. Empathy means coming to know, to value, and to respect another person from that person's frame of reference, "seeing it their way, through their eyes" without necessarily agreeing or disagreeing with what they are saying.

Empathy, the ability to share in another's emotions or feelings, will become the focus of intense scientific study during the 1990's because it is among the most socially desirable of personality traits, the bedrock of both a sense of justice and of concern for the welfare of others.

Daniel Goleman

You have probably heard the expression, "put yourself in the other person's shoes." This does not mean you must try to become that other person. Matter of fact, that is impossible and usually impedes communication. Rather, when you have empathic understanding of another person, you have an awareness of that person's internal frame of reference. However, you do not need to jeopardize your own frame of reference to understand another's. In empathic understanding you are *"with"* that person, but you do not *"become"* that person. You're "reading" that person, feeling that you know and understand what is being experienced. In addition, you sense that that person knows you are attempting to be understanding, although you probably will never wholly comprehend all of what that person is experiencing.

More than anything else, your attempts to perceive feelings tell people you are *trying* to understand them, regardless of whether your statements are accurate. However, the more accurate the empathy, the better. Communicating empathic understanding puts a *"chip in the bank"* towards the development of a nonthreatening, facilitative relationship. "Chip in the bank" statements help create the bond needed for effective communication. However, the *attempt* at understanding also puts a "chip in the bank." So, you really can't lose using this model in attempting better communication; you always get "credit" for trying to understand the other person. That is, even if you "miss," the person realizes your *genuine,* authentic interest and will "fill you in"—communication is always enhanced by attempted empathy.

He drew a circle that shut me out-

Heretic, rebel, a thing to flout-

But Love and I had the wit to win:

We drew a circle that took him in.

Edwin Markham

Although listening is essential in facilitative communication, it is not sufficient in itself. Even the most "interested" and attentive person may have difficulty helping another unless listening results in understanding. This implies the need for actions on your part. However, understanding involves more than assuming another person's role for a brief time. Effective understanding is recognizing and describing, usually verbally, but not necessarily in detail, the thoughts and feelings of others.

The word "empathy" is often used as a synonym for "understanding." However, as noted, empathy implies that you not only understand the ideas expressed, but that you have identified the feelings present. If you can "tune in" to others, you will experience a closeness that enables you to know them better. You will feel like you are really with them, and "good vibes" will be generated. You will not only be sensitive to their words, but also to the feelings that accompany those words. Empathy provides a meaningful experience for the person talking, and also a unique and rewarding experience for you, the listener. You will learn more about this skill in the next chapter.

Everyone can come to know themselves and their feelings better through empathic understanding on the part of others. Letting them know we are trying to understand also provides opportunities for self-initiated change if it is desired. Unfortunately, there is considerable evidence that empathic understanding is not a typical characteristic of the general population, and, to my knowledge, no one cultural group has a monopoly on being empathic. However, empathic understanding is an interpersonal skill which can be taught, learned, and acquired through practice. As noted, you will learn more about how to acquire this skill in the next chapter.

Facilitative Communicators are Respectful

Respect for others means accepting their experiences as important parts of their lives. We show respect for individuals when we acknowledge them as persons with human potential for joys, depressions, successes, and failures, regardless of their respective race, religion, gender, or cultural background. To respect another person as a human being implies that we value that person's feelings and worth (but not necessarily the behaviors). Thus, true respect indicates concern for the person as a unique person with unique feelings and experiences. Showing respect allows us to go beyond our stereotypes, for example, to search for the *real* person rather than approving or disapproving of the individual's thoughts or behaviors. If we feel and show our respect (i.e., unconditional positive regard) for others, they can and will feel closer to us.

Do you know when you are respected? Another way of showing respect is to let others "do it their way." If someone is always telling you "how to do" a certain thing, that person probably does not respect you or your ability.

Respect goes beyond optimism or simple reassurance. It is the communication of deep interest and concern. A high regard for others emphasizes that their dignity, worth, culture, and feelings are accepted and valued, and that they are not being judged. The degree to which a person communicates respect for another defines the relationship, as well as the limits of what can be freely explored in that relationship.

Some individuals have low self-respect caused in part by previous experiences where their feelings and thoughts were not accepted or valued. When such people begin to experience respect, they stop "defending" themselves long enough to examine new patterns of living and thinking. Thus, your positive regard, warmth, and respect help to break down the barriers of isolation, and pave the way for communication as well as new self-esteem on the part of others.

Facilitative Communicators Know the Culturally Different

As mentioned throughout this book, a culturally skilled, facilitative communicator is willing to gain cognitive knowledge about different cultures, i.e., their history, cultural values, current problems, lifestyles, and so forth. This may be the most important thing we can do in becoming more effective intercultural communicators.

It is important that we approach different cultural members with understanding over and above our feelings. That is, having strong feelings of support for a particular culture and its participants is necessary. However, it is not enough to truly communicate with participants from that cultural group. If we are ignorant of the values and ways of participants from cultural groups different from ours, we will certainly be less effective communicators than we would be if we operated with accurate, cognitive understanding of them.

Individual disparities and differences are compounded when we have a lack of knowledge about culturally distinct groups. If we function only within the framework of our own congenial, familiar cultural situations, we may be prone to impose idealized values on others. We all have the right to express our values, but not to impose them on others!

A basic reason for the lack of understanding of other cultures is the prescriptions about American behavior. To a great extent, our standards of conduct and morality have been determined and "enforced" by middle and upper-class Anglos. And, as noted, ordinary middle-class Anglos often get caught up in the notion of assumed similarity. That is, they may feel that everyone is like them, or should be; therefore, communication is one-way and distorted. Those individuals with a sound knowledge of another's culture and environment will more likely understand the sources and reasons for some behaviors that may even have appeared odd or peculiar prior to gaining such knowledge.

Facilitative Communicators are Aware of Their Own Assumptions, Values, and Biases

In addition to knowledge of different cultural groups, cultur-ally skilled, facilitative communicators are aware of their own assumptions, values, and biases regarding different groups of people. What assumptions do you hold regarding people who are different from you? What biases? It is important that we work through any biases or prejudices we may have about *any* and all groups of people. Such a personal, self-examination can be emotionally difficult, and for some people, a painful process. We have all been told that "facing the truth about yourself will set you free," and/or "know yourself." However, the truth can also be personally painful!

Do you view other cultures as equally valuable to yours? Is your cultural group superior to another? Are you culturally sensitive to your own heritage and the possibility that you were taught (perhaps unconsciously) to be prejudiced as a part of your upbringing? Do you value and respect differences? Are you aware of your own values and biases and how they affect those who are culturally different? Do you avoid stereotyping and labeling? Do you monitor your own assumptions about those different from you? Are you willing to accept someone of a different race into your organization, i.e., your sorority, your fraternity, your church? It is important that each of us examine ourselves concerning these questions if we hope to become culturally skilled commu-nicators.

Facilitative Persons Value the Learning of and Using Facilitative Communication Skills

As noted in the preface of this book, much of what society is and much of what it will become is contingent upon our effectiveness in establishing interpersonal relationships with those culturally different as well as with those who are similar to us—valuing diversity and sameness. People are a vital part of our lives. We need others in order to be fulfilled as persons and to experience all of our human potential. In fact, much of what we are and what we will become is a result of our interactions with others. When our interpersonal relationships are positive and open, we experience our "humanness" and move toward personal fulfillment. We learn, and we help others to learn. We feel alive and we enjoy life. On the other hand, when our relationships lack personal involvement or when they restrict our personal growth, we feel "inhumaneness" that is reflected in a joyless existence. The facilitative communicator knows that effective interpersonal communication skills are needed if others are to be assisted positively toward self-enhancement. Moreover, the facilitative communicator knows that effective interpersonal skills do not just happen by chance; they are learned.

A few fortunate people, albeit very few, have been raised in family environments where effective interpersonal communication skills were a common part of their lives. Parent and sibling use of such skills not only facilitated their own personal growth, but it also helped them be facilitative in interactions with others. These people usually display the characteristics of facilitative communicators noted previously. More often than not, because their parents or significant others in their lives responded to them in facilitative ways, they learned—through modeling and/or experience—valuable skills for effective interpersonal communication. However, even these people can benefit from careful examination of evidence accumulated about interpersonal relationships and communication, especially when they want to improve their effectiveness in working with others who are different from them. The few exceptions noted above notwithstanding, most people lack models to help them learn, or experiences to help them appreciate, the value of interpersonal communication skills. That is, the vast majority of us need help in developing and using communication skills that facilitate personal growth in others.

Genuineness, Warmth, Personal Regard, and Empathic understanding are the core of interpersonal relationships. Whether teacher, parent, friend, or stranger, these qualities have no preference by age, culture, social, or economic status. They are the best of being human in making contact with others. These attitudes facilitate relationships, growth, and learning.

Melvin Witmer

Facilitative people are sensitive to the impact of words on individuals. Sometimes our words are "weapons" which harm our relationships, especially with individuals from a different culture. Effective communicators are interested in a language of feelings as well as ideas. Facilitators know that although nonverbal communication plays an important role in relationships, verbal communication is the critical factor. They know that words reflect attitudes and feelings as much as ideas do. A few carefully chosen words communicate an invitation to talk, to risk, and to come (psychologically and/or socially) closer. Ill-chosen words are hurtful, push people away, close communication, threaten relationships, and cause defensiveness.

Have you ever been in a situation where you were with a person, listening intently to what was being said, and suddenly feeling that you really understood what the person was saying and feeling? Then, just as suddenly, you were wondering and thinking, "What can I say now? I'm at a loss for words." *Perhaps* no words were necessary. *Perhaps* your being an effective listener was helpful enough. *Perhaps* your genuine interest and respect were somehow communicated through your gestures, eye contact, or other nonverbal cues. But, *perhaps* some words could have been said that would have communicated your caring, respect, and understanding even more effectively.

Facilitative individuals know that good communication can not be taken for granted, and that most people do not have a full repertoire of effective interpersonal skills. Good communication between people cannot be left to chance, not if real caring is present. Fortunately, good communication can result from learning facilitative communication skills. Such skills are the focus of the remainder of this book.

Individual Practice Activity

Think of an individual—an individual you remember fondly as having had a positive impact on you when you were younger. If you can, think about those school days when you were in elementary, junior, or senior high school. Select a person who stands out in your mind as someone who helped you. Do you have someone in mind? Okay, now write a word or phrase below that best describes that person. There may be many words or phrases, but write just *one*. What is the one most important characteristic that person possessed? Write the word(s) now:

Positive impact word/phrase _____

Now, think of an individual who had a negative impact on you when you were younger. This is the kind of person with whom you would not want to spend another day! There may be more than one. Pick one person. Now, write a word or phrase that describes that person. Do not write the person's name.

Negative impact word/phrase _____

Did the words you wrote describe the personal characteristics of the two individuals? Did you describe your "favorite" with terms such as brilliant, knowledgeable, studious, or as having a particular degree, or as being of certain age, sex, race, or nationality? Words such as these are almost always missing from such discussions. Rather, the words used tend to focus upon personal, emotional characteristics.

You were probably affected positively by individuals who were caring, understanding, and interested in your ideas. They were good listeners, had a sense of humor, and respected you as a person. Most likely, negative, non-facilitative individuals tended to be described as sarcastic, cold, judgmental, unaccepting, self-centered, insensitive, distant, punitive, and arbitrary. Perhaps we should ask ourselves, "How do others perceive us? How do we want others to describe us?"

Group Practice Activity

Instructor's Note:

Divide the participants into small groups of 5 or 6. Ask each group to select a discussion leader. Give the groups about 10 minutes, during which time each person tells about the individuals (negative and positive referents) described above *without naming them.* Before beginning, instruct the small group leaders to use the guidelines presented previously for leading group discussions. When they finish, you might lead a large group discussion based on the ideas presented above.

Outside Assignment

Think of three friends and take note of how they act around you. What three words would they use to describe you? Write them down. Now identify three past friends who caused you difficulties or concerns. What three words would each of them use to describe you? Complete this exercise when alone. Be prepared to discuss these descriptions with a small group at your next group/class meeting.

Example 1:

Assume you are talking with a friend, Priscilla, who is culturally different from you and attending college (while living at home). You want to know about her vocational interests and future plans. Priscilla says to you, "I'm really interested in going to graduate school to study interior design, but there are none close by. I don't want to leave home and go away to college just yet." How would you respond in this situation? What would be your first response (words) to her?

You want to communicate as facilitatively as possible. Several possible responses are listed below. Rank order them (in your opinion) from most facilitative to least facilitative. Place a 1 beside your most facilitative response, a 2 beside your next most facilitative response, and so on to 7, the least facilitative response.

_____ a. You shouldn't be afraid to go away from home to graduate school. That may just be your culture. It's time for you to leave home and it would be good for you.

_____ b. What is it about leaving home that concerns you most?

_____ c. You're concerned about being away from your family.

_____ d. Going away could be fun and you'll probably enjoy it after awhile.

_____ e. Right now you don't want to leave your family and go away to graduate school.

_____ f. Don't you like living away from home?

_____ g. You don't want to leave home because you've never been away from your family before.

Now, let us try again. Your goal is to make a facilitative statement to a friend—a statement that will be perceived as facilitative and helpful. Read over the possible responses below and again rank order them from one to seven; from 1 for that response you consider to be the most understanding and facilitative to 7, the one you consider least facilitative.

Example 2:

Carlos, your roommate, returns to school from a weekend at home and says he wishes he had a home like others. He reports, sadly, that his parents fight a lot. He doesn't know what to do. He has heard his parents arguing and worries that his father may leave home and not come back. And, their arguing is really affecting his school work.

____a. What do you do when you hear your parents arguing?

____ b. Hearing your parents argue frightens you and its having a negative impact on your studies.

____ c. Hearing your parents argue makes you realize how dependent you are on them, and you're wondering just how much they do care for you.

____ d. Try to get more involved in your schoolwork and don't go home so often. It might help to take your mind off the problems at home, and you'll feel better.

____ e. There's nothing wrong with parents getting upset with one another, or your being concerned. I'd probably feel the way you do too.

____ f. You're thinking that your family is not like other families in that they fight more than most.

____ g. Do they argue all the time?

My Rankings

Example 1:

a. 7; b. 3; c. 1; d. 5; e. 2; f. 4 g. 6

Example 2:

a. 3; b. 1; c. 6; d. 7; e. 5; f. 2 g. 4

Did my rankings surprise you? How did your rankings compare with how I responded to Priscilla and Carlos? Regardless, do not worry about how you ranked the responses in the two examples. As you continue with the next chapter, my rankings will make more sense to you. And, you will have another opportunity to respond to Carlos and Priscilla later.

Outside Activity

Read the poem below, respond to the questions following it, and be prepared to discuss your responses.

Listening

When I ask you to listen to me and you start giving advice, you have not done what I asked.

When I ask you to listen to me and you begin to tell me why I shouldn't feel that way, you are trampling on my feelings.

When I ask you to listen to me and you feel you have to do something to solve my problem, you have failed me, strange as that may seem.

Listen! All I ask was that you listen, not talk, or do anything... just hear.

Advice is cheap: twenty-five cents will get you both Dear Abby and Billy Graham in the same newspaper.

And I can do for myself. I'm not helpless. Maybe discouraged and faltering, but not helpless.

When you do something for me that I can and need to do for myself, you contribute to my fear and inadequacy.

But when you accept, as a simple fact, that I do feel, no matter how irrational, then I can quit trying to convince you and get about the business of understanding what's behind this irrational feeling.

And when that's clear, the answers are obvious and I don't need advice. Irrational feelings make sense when we understand what's behind them.

So please listen and just hear me. And if you want to talk, wait a minute for your turn, and I'll listen to you.

Ray Houghton, M.D.

1. What struck you most about the poem?
2. What does reading the poem make you want to change about your own listening habits?
3. What implications does the poem have for intercultural communication?

Chapter X

Verbal Responses: From Least to Most Facilitative

In the previous chapter, I presented several characteristics that best describe facilitative communicators. Are these just "nice" theory words or can these characteristics be taught? Except for "genuineness," the answer is "yes." And, it is a fact that certain types of verbal responses, if given genuinely, result in others perceiving us as being more facilitative. The use of other responses in our conversations make us less facilitative communicators. This chapter is about responding verbally to others, or specifically, it is about the ways and words we can use to respond, and how such responses influence others' perceptions of us.

As noted, current research indicates that certain verbal responses tend to be perceived by others as more facilitative. That is, certain verbal responses convey more interest, empathy, caring, warmth, acceptance, and understanding, and are more person-centered than other responses. Such responses, therefore, have a higher probability of creating a facilitative interpersonal relationship with those different and/or similar. Skill in the use of these facilitative responses is the key to becoming effective in communication with others, regardless of race or cultural background mixes.

Any response made in a conversation has an impact on the person(s) hearing the response. This impact invariably affects the response receiver's general perception of the person making the response. From what a respondent says, people gain impressions used not only to formulate their own responses, but they also gain understanding of the relationship with the respondent. Therefore, it is important to understand the probable impact of certain responses.

From studies of verbal behavior in counseling, psychotherapy, communication, and teaching, there emerges a set of responses that can be categorized as more facilitative than others. That is, your using them keeps the conversation flowing. These responses enhance the desire of others to continue talking—their use makes it "easier" for them to continue. These response categories are: *open-ended questioning, clarifying and summarizing,* and *tuning in to the feelings of others.*

On the other hand, there are many and varied responses that impede communication; i.e., they are "communication stoppers." Some of these responses are more prevalent in certain cultures than others. However, it is my opinion that several such less-facilitative responses are cross-cultural in nature and more common than others. They are: *untimely advice; judgment or evaluation; analyzing or interpreting another's behavior, actions, or personality; inappropriate reassurance or support;* and *non-facilitative type questions (the soliciting agreement question, the forced choice question, the double bind question, the closed question,* and *the why question).*

These are covered in more detail below.

It is not my intent to imply that these latter responses should never be used. However, decreasing the frequency of their use and using them only in a timely, appropriate, fashion will result in you being more facilitative in communication with others. On the other hand, increasing the frequency of the more facilitative responses *(open-ended questions, clarification,* and *tuning in to feelings)* increases the chances of our being perceived as more facilitative communicators.

Any of the several responses listed above may be "facilitative" at one time or another. However, they are ranked here (in reverse order, 7 to 1—most facilitative) because of their *probable* respective effect in establishing a helpful, facilitative interpersonal relationship with others both similar and different. The discussion of each of these responses that follows is in reverse order of their facilitative value.

7. Untimely Advising/Evaluating

6. Interpreting/Analyzing

5. Inappropriate Reassurance/Support

4. Non-Facilitative Questioning

   a. Soliciting Agreement

   b. Forced Choice

   c. Double Bind

   d. Closed

   e. Why

3. Open-Ended Questioning

2. Clarifying/Summarizing

1. Tuning In To Feelings

Advising and Evaluating (7)

At one time or another, all of us have felt that we know enough information about a particular subject that we consider ourselves to be "experts" or authorities. For example, a man who has been selling life insurance for fifteen years is likely to consider himself an expert on the subject. Similarly, a woman who has been teaching a college philosophy course for five years might consider herself to be an authority on philosophy. Each of us also may consider ourselves experts in other areas such as raising children, growing rare Japanese ferns, sewing, painting, playing cards, or home repairs—any of a number of things. In a like manner, people create the image that their ideas are *most valuable,* and that they should be questioned seldom if ever.

Thus, because each of us likes to consider ourselves to be an authority on different topics, it is easy to understand our tendency to respond to others seeking our assistance by giving information as advice.

Think about your own method of responding to others. Do you almost always "agree" or "disagree" verbally (or non-verbally) with what the other person just said? Is this a form of evaluation?

Think about it. Sometimes it is better to acknowledge what was just said than to agree or disagree with the statement that was just made.

When we assume an "advising" role and do most of the talking in interacting with a person who makes a request of us, it is likely that we are viewed as a person "hard to talk to," a poor communicator and listener, and a low facilitator of others. Facilitative communicators are more concerned with others' thoughts, ideas, and feelings than simply what they can tell other people.

Advice is information given by someone who can't use it to someone who won't.

Anonymous

Untimely advising and evaluating responses indicate judgment of another's relative goodness, appropriateness, effectiveness, or rightness within the responder's own value structure. They imply what the other individual might, ought to, or should do. Here are some examples:

"I know you don't like college, but you'll be able to get a better job when you graduate."

"You never have accepted Blacks. What you need to do is forget the past."

"Instead of arguing, you should try to understand your parents' point of view."

"You still think all Indians are drunkards, don't you? Well, what you should do is visit a reservation."

"If you would study more, your parents wouldn't be so upset with you."

"Give your instructors some credit. If I were you, I would look at the positive side."

"Why don't you just tell him to back off or you'll never go out with him?"

"You had better come down hard now or he will take advantage of you later."

"What you need to do is to go talk to your boss. She might not be as unfair as you think."

Joe Wittmer, Ph.D.

"Getting along with those different from you has always been your shortcoming. What you need to do is...."

"You never have understood money. The best thing to do is to sell it now and invest the money in an IRA account."

It should be acknowledged that certain traditional, cultural group participants may be more likely to seek your advice than are others. For example, Sue and Sue (1990) indicated that Asians and Hispanics often seek advice and suggestions from others. However, Sue and Sue also stated that "getting right to the point" with Native Americans may be seen as rude or immature behavior. In addition, Littlejohn and Henderson (Chapter 5) indicated that the evaluation of an African American, especially by a non-African American, will quickly halt the conversation between the two. Thus, I suggest that the "safest" and most facilitative conversing method may be to avoid *untimely* advice and evaluation at all times, regardless of whether the person is similar or different from you. However, we all need *timely* advice from time to time and we *all* give such advice to others from time to time. Timely advice does not negatively affect the relationship, but is best received when preceded by interest in and/or acceptance of, the person to whom we are about to give it.

Many receive advice, few profit by it.

Publius Syrius

Advising and evaluating responses are easily identified because they *tell people how to behave or what to do.* Unfortunately, although most of us use such responses to try to give helpful advice, there is great likelihood that the advice given is a projection of our own needs, problems, or values. A common example is, "If I were you...." People *may* follow your advice, but then later find that it was not valid for them. Notice how the following statement leads tend to influence another person's thinking:

"The best solution is...."

"Why don't you...."

"You should...."

"You ought to...."

"You need..."

"If I were you...."

"If you would just..."

"The thing to do is...."

"The best way is...."

"If you don't, then...."

Advice is received and given by almost everyone almost every day. Listen to any conversation, whether in a business or social setting, and notice how often people offer advice when an individual suggests concern about something. And, as noted, when advice is relevant, logical, and practical, it can be helpful in communication with others, particularly if it is offered at an appropriate time (i.e., at a time when it is received as a suggestion rather than as a command: "Have you thought about maybe..." or, "What about the possibility of going....") In order to be helpful, advice should not be offered when people are rebelling or being defensive. To be helpful, advice should be given at a time when individuals feel that they can and will accept responsibilities for their decisions and subsequent behaviors. Also, as noted, advice giving is appropriate if proceeded by understanding; then it is much more likely to be appreciated and accepted at face value.

Professional counselors and psychotherapists are often skeptical of advice giving because it shifts the responsibility for problem solving from the person to the professional counselor or therapist, i.e., "I tried what you told me to do and it didn't work." Such an approach limits the person's opportunity to make changes and robs him or her of the satisfaction of personal resolution. For example, teachers know the value of the "discovery method" of teaching because it encourages children to accept responsibility for their own learning and actions. They also realize that lecturing is (basically) contradictory to the discovery learning method. Similarly, good communicators know that advice giving is contradictory to people solving their own problems. Effective counselors realize that the most they can be is a *catalyst* in indirectly helping the person with a personal problem. Like you, counselors do not own "magic wands."

Another problem of advice giving is that it is often perceived as threatening, because advice giving (which is usually preceded by some form of evaluation, i.e., "I know what's wrong with you, you're...; what you need to do is...") is often perceived as criticism.

Consequently, untimely advice and evaluation responses frequently result in hesitation, resistance, rejection, and inaction in the people to whom we are talking.

Assume a person evaluates you negatively for driving a small, "gas saving" foreign car, and you in turn judge that person negatively for driving a large "gas guzzling," American car. As long as you judge or evaluate one another's ownerships of such cars, you probably will never fully understand each other's perceptions and values about automobiles, or why you drive the cars you drive! Your individual perceptions and feelings about cars will only pull further apart if you continue to judge each other for owning the respective types of automobiles. Further, the more you judge another person for the car he or she drives, the more the other person will defend driving a particular type of car! Both of you are apt to engage in "yea, but..." activity. The same applies to human traits—the more we judge, evaluate (or nag) people to change personal characteristics or behaviors, the more apt they are to respond to you, and reveal to you, that, "that's the way they are." Untimely evaluating or judging statements cause others to "defend" themselves, and open communication is impossible.

Imagine that your perceptions, and the person's to whom you are talking, are like two giant circles. In order to understand one another fully, our respective perceptions (our respective "circles") of an event, situation, behavior, or characteristic must *overlap* significantly so that we achieve commonality of meaning. We do this by conveying non-judgmental understanding of the feelings and perceptions behind our respective perceptions. To achieve an overlap of respective perceptions (our circles), we both must feel *non-threatened* and *non-defensive* in our communications. The more defensive or threatened we feel, the further apart our "circles" will grow! Untimely evaluation and advice does not allow for feelings of interpersonal comfortableness in which threat and defensiveness are absent.

Yet another problem of untimely advising and evaluating is that it disrupts the flow of communication. When people project their value systems through judging, evaluating, or untimely advice giving, the people being spoken to begin to think defensively. For example, unconsciously or consciously, people feeling defensive say things such as:

"She won't like what I'm going to say now."

"He's going to think that I'm...."

"She wants me to...."

"He won't understand me."

"I should... if I want her to like me."

If advice and evaluation are given in the attempt to motivate others, there is a tendency for them to feel that specific expectations must be met if they are to be of value. They believe they must continue to "produce" for the person giving advice in order to maintain attention, acceptance, and respect.

If you doubt the effect advice or evaluation have upon individuals, check it out by giving someone some "good" advice, and then notice the person's reaction. Most likely the first few words uttered will be something such as, "Yes, but..." or, "That's a good idea, however...." Relatedly, take note of your own feelings and reactions the next time someone gives you "good" advice or evaluates you, i.e., "You didn't like that movie? What's wrong with you? You need to loosen up a little—go with the flow."

There is no way around it. Untimely or poorly given advice and evaluation, especially to our peers, are low facilitators of communication. They do little, if anything, to establish a facilitative relationship with another, especially if that person is culturally different. Further, when over used, advice and evaluation responses may even create (feelings of) dependency.

Again, to reiterate, this does not mean that advice should never be given; all of us have benefited from "good" advice at one time or another. However, advice has a positive impact on others only when it is timely and relevant.

Rather than giving advice or judgment, a facilitative person opens the flow of communication by first thinking, "I need to know how that person sees the event or situation, rather than sharing my own value judgment at this time. I can best communicate with this person by exploring the situation, alternatives, and consequences, as they appear to him or her rather than telling him or her whether the behavior was right or wrong, i.e., maybe ask; "What was it about the movie that you didn't like?" instead of evaluating him or her for differing with your perception of the movie. Alternatively, the facilitative person might reason, "I can be a better communicator by encouraging him or her to examine his or her own ideas further and by clarifying the situation." Facilitative communicators realize that while giving advice is expedient, careful listening and appropriate responding have much greater impact and benefit.

Be aware of your own tendency to evaluate ("I know what's wrong with you") and advise ("And, this is what you ought to do!") in an untimely manner. Jumping into a conversation to inform someone that he or she has a certain "problem" and "fixing" it immediately is not facilitative at *anytime*. And, psychologists imply that we are more prone to evaluate those individuals and/or groups to whom we judge ourselves superior, i.e., we think they cannot do it without our help; we do not respect their ability. This has tremendous implications for individuals who believe that their culture is somehow better than another's and that the latter needs to "change" to be acceptable.

Untimely advice and evaluation are among the most commonly used responses in everyday interactions and, in my view, are among the least facilitative, especially when attempting to communicate with someone from a different cultural or racial background.

Analyzing and Interpreting (6)

Some people think that they can be helpful by analyzing (and subsequently "explaining") a situation for another person. Perhaps this response gained its popularity from the theory that there are "always" logical reasons why people do things. Consider these responses:

"Don't you see, that particular professor is like your father. They both are authority figures and they trigger rebellion in you."

"You did that because of the way you were raised in your culture."

"This frustration on the job stems from your lack of success with your marriage."

"It's really apparent to me that the reason you are angry is because it's easier to get angry than to talk to her about what happened."

"I know why you did that, it is traditional in your group."

"You sit there and don't contribute to the conversation because you're afraid people will not accept you because of your race."

In each of these examples, the (probably well-intentioned) motive is to explain, analyze, or interpret the other person's behavior as opposed to focusing on and trying to understand the person's perceptions or feelings at the time the response was being made. Sometimes effort is made to connect one event to another, by giving analyzing and interpreting responses, in the hope that the connection will give the person insight which will lead to behavior change. However, analyzing or interpreting responses imply what the person *ought to think*. Such responses may also be viewed as condescending to participants of other cultures, or "insults" by implying that the person was not smart enough to figure out the connection. They are intended to explain ideas, events, or situations, but they often generate negative reactions.

How do you feel when someone tries to analyze or interpret your behavior? Chances are you do not like it. Most of us dislike the idea that another person is implying that he or she knows us better, knows more about ourselves than we do, has more knowledge about *our culture* than we ourselves have, i.e., "You're self-conscious about your background because...." We shy away from individuals who act as if they know us better than we know ourselves!

Sometimes a person making an interpretation is accurate, but most of the time the person is only guessing. Too many times an analytic statement tends to be a "textbook interpretation," a "generalized analysis." For example, consider the statement, "Thedrice, when you don't get what you want from Mary Ann, you call up Cyndy to make Mary Ann jealous, and that's why you never get it together with Mary Ann." This statement *might* be accurate. However, the person is most likely only guessing what really motivated Thedrice. Maybe the talker really likes Cyndy too, and is having a hard time choosing between them, in which case the jealousy issue may not be very important.

Have you ever had a person say to you, "You know why you did that? Well, let me tell you...." If you could remember your reaction at that time, there is a good chance that you withdrew coldly. No one likes to view him or herself as an entry in a textbook. While the amateur analyst is hoping for an "ah ha," most of the time all that person gets is an "uh huh" or "nope" because such statements provoke defensiveness—even among the best of friends.

A danger in making an analyzing or interpreting response is that we project our attitudes, values, and feelings on the other person. This will especially hinder our efforts in communicating with someone who is culturally different from us. Interpretation impedes open communication by emphasizing personal interpretation of another's world rather than showing interest in learning about that person's world. And, the ability to "see" another's worldview and the acceptance of it, is, in my opinion, the key to intercultural communication. Even effective counselors and therapists do not rely heavily on these types of statements to facilitate personal growth or rapport. The facilitative communicator is interested in helping others become more aware of that which they are experiencing rather than attempting to explain reasons behind behavior.

Inappropriate Reassurance and Support (5)

Reassurance and support involve statements intended to tell other people we believe in them. They are designed to be a "pat on the back" to help someone keep going. And, given appropriately, they can be powerful. Unfortunately, inappropriate reassuring and supporting responses often imply that individuals "need not *feel* as they do." That is, the tendency is to dismiss feelings as being "normal" or "common" and that the person need not be concerned or feel differently.

Consider these responses:

"Oh, well, everyone feels like that on occasion."

"Hey, everything's going to turn out okay."

"You know, you're not much different from us Anglos in that respect."

"Relax! Everything's going to be okay."

"All mothers are like that."

"You have a lot in common with this guy I know. He...."

"Things look bad now, but as soon as...."

"I know exactly how you feel."

Timely encouragement and support can be helpful. Educators are often admonished to "catch a child being good," and then reinforce the child with encouragement. Encouragement can build self-confidence, increase security, motivate learning, generate good will, and improve human relations. However, if "support statements" come across as insincere flattery, they have little or no impact, i.e., " I really like your culture, some of my best friends are...." Interestingly, even some sincere statements of support result in other than what was intended. For example, suppose that the following statements were made to you: "You are such a great person. You're probably the best person I know." At first glance it may seem these statements would make you feel more confident and appreciated. However, you might also find yourself becoming a little defensive. "Ah, you are just saying that to make me feel good!" Or, "Really? Well, I do try, but I'm not always sure how it will turn out."

Certain cultural groups also respond to, and use praise, support, and reassurance differently than others. For example, the culture in which I was reared (the Old Order Amish) do not praise children individually, they praise the group. Thus, my father used to request of me, "Joe, clean the barn." And, when the task was completed, he would comment simply, "Joe, the barn is now clean!" Can you imagine being an Amish child in a public elementary school classroom, as the writer was, where individual praise flourishes? Can you clearly see, from this example and others, the necessity for learning (cognitive empathy) about other cultural groups?

Sometimes inappropriate compliments create discomfort and make us feel less confident. It is not easy to handle praise, especially when it focuses on and evaluates our personality: "You are such a good person." "You are always so thoughtful and sensitive." Or, "You are always pleasant to be around and never say an unkind word." Praise of this nature makes us feel uneasy, even though initially it seems pleasant.

---

*Praise that evaluates personality and character is unpleasant, unsafe. Praise that describes **efforts, accomplishments, and feelings** is helpful and safe.... **Describe**, don't evaluate. Deal with events, don't appraise personality. Describe feelings, don't **evaluate** character. Give a realistic picture of the accomplishment, don't glorify the person.*

Haim Ginott

When we describe behaviors or events and our specific feelings related to them, as opposed to focusing on their personality, the people receiving the praise draw their own conclusions.

For example, as a result of expressing our positive feelings and being specific about behavior, a person may conclude, "I am liked, respected, appreciated, capable, and valued."

Suppose a *close* friend that you haven't seen for a while (who has very obviously gained a lot of weight since you last saw this person) says to you; "I gained so much weight over the summer. Look at me, I'm fat!" What would you say? It would be difficult not to give reassurance in this situation, i.e., "Oh, you didn't gain that much, I think you look pretty good." However, it might be more appropriate and timely to recognize your friend's *concern* (be empathic) in this situation at this time. Recognizing the concern would most likely facilitate your friend to continue verbalizing feelings, to continue sharing with you. The inappropriate reassurance statement offered above would most certainly imply, "Don't feel that way," and would probably cause a quick change in the subject being discussed. It implies that you really do not want to hear any more negative feelings at this time.

In sum, support and reassurance responses given timely are good responses to give others. However, such responses often tell someone "not to feel that way," or worse, they shut off others' feelings because we appear to be saying to them, "Don't share anymore of your negative feelings with me," and thus may not be conducive to better interpersonal communication. Use such responses in an appropriate and timely fashion.

Non-Facilitative Type Questions (4)

A lot has been written about questions and the process of questioning. In fact, the "art" of questioning often has been thought to be the central part of the communication process. Books have been written about questioning strategies.

There is no doubt that questioning is a valuable tool in the communication process. However, most people tend to ask too many questions. "Bombarding" our friends with questions can be a frightening experience for them. It is much like facing a prosecuting attorney who asks questions in order to trap witnesses. Too many questions make people feel uneasy and defensive, and it makes them wonder why they should answer such a threatening person. However, a question can be a facilitative response when used to obtain information, stimulate further discussion, or query an individual regarding a particular matter to reveal your genuine "interest" in what is being said. A question implies one will profit further by developing a point of discussion. It also opens other areas of discussion. An effective question encourages people to share information.

A person usually tries to give the kind of response that will satisfy the person asking a question. Sometimes this leads to a quick question-and-answer pattern, an interaction which impedes spontaneous discussion. The mode of questioning determines the scope and depth of the information being collected, and the pace of the discussion.

If people are willing to submit to a "cross-examination," they assume the procedure will be productive, and that questioning is the only way to solve the problem. However, people also assume that we have all the "answers." If we cannot solve a problem, then why ask all the questions? Too many questions also may lead some to believe they have been "tricked" into revealing information. Certain types of questions also may put people "on-guard."

We all need to ask questions to get along with our lives and questioning is an important part of any interpersonal process. Here are some things to keep in mind to use questions appropriately:

1. What is the purpose of the question?
2. What kinds of questions are available?
3. What alternative response might be used instead of a question?
4. What impact will the questions have on the relationship?

Certain questions can be painful and/or threatening, especially if they probe too deeply too quickly. Questions also can make people feel inadequate; they can misdirect thinking about the meaning that something has for them.

In addition, participants from certain cultural groups may not respond, and/or be "turned off" by certain types of questions. For example, Sue and Sue (1990) wrote that Native Americans may consider personal questions as "prying." In addition, an African American expert on intercultural communication informed me that asking personal questions of an African American, whom you have just met (for the first time) is viewed as intrusive and improper. And, as Littlejohn and Henderson stated (Chapter 5), probing an African American may impede communication.

Joe Wittmer, Ph.D.

Following are some types of questions that have low probability for facilitating effective interpersonal communication.

A. **The Soliciting Agreement Question.** Sometimes a question is asked which requires an answer, but it suggests that the response must be in agreement with the questioner's point of view. To answer such a question any differently would only provoke argument or disagreement. For example:

"You don't really think you've finished that job, do you?"

"Not being on time is sort of okay with your people, isn't it?"

"You know she didn't mean that remark, right? Some of her best friends are Black."

"You didn't mean what you said about Jim, did you?"

"She really works hard at being a good friend and you know that, don't you?"

B. **The Forced-Choice Question.** This type of question is "either-or" because it limits the respondent's choice. The respondent might prefer none of the choices, but is forced to choose from what has been offered. For example:

"Do you want to do your homework now in the library or do it this evening at the apartment?"

"Are you going to sit and pout all morning or are you going to go tell him how you really feel?"

"When are you going to stop feeling sorry for yourself?"

Unfortunately, this kind of question is used far too often and by too many. It often is used when we are in a hurry, or when we have limited alternatives. Regardless, it is a poor type of question because it gives others no opportunity to share their own perceptions of the matter.

C. **The Double Bind Question.** Another type of notoriously poor question is the double bind question in which the respondent is judged, no matter which way the question is answered. For example:

"Have you stopped calling him names?"

"Have you quit smoking again?"

"Have you stopped using drugs?"

"Doesn't that just happen naturally to whites?"

"What do you people really want?"

"Are you still in love with Debbie?"

D. **Closed Questions.** The closed question is structured basically for only a "yes" or "no" response. It can usually be answered in a few words and, thus, it is seldom facilitative. That is, such questions do not create "flow" in a conversation. Consider the following from the respondent's perspective:

"Do you like Lionel a lot?"

"Did you like reading that section?"

"Are you ready for the test?"

"Do you get along with Hispanics?"

A closed question forces people to answer in terms of the questioning person's perceptual field and tends to seek cold yes-no responses. For example:

"You really don't like Asians, do you?"

"Is this the part that's upsetting you?"

"Did the fact that she called you a racist upset you?"

E. **The Why Question.** The "why" question is another type of question that deserves special attention. Most people really do not know *why* they do some of the things they do. Do people on drugs really know why they started? Does a person who tells jokes about other cultural groups know why it is fun to tell them? In addition, in many cultures the word "why" tends to connote disapproval or displeasure. Most likely, regardless of our cultural background, we were reprimanded, judged, or shown some sign of disapproval through "why" questions, such as the following:

"Why do you always have to come through the front door?"

"Why don't you hang up your clothes?"

"Why don't you learn to speak English better?"

"Why do you date someone so different from you?"

"Why don't you study more?"

"Why are you late?"

"Why do you want to run around with Blacks?"

Remember? As we grew up we found ways to defend ourselves against this kind of question. We learned that the person asking the question was not really interested in the reasons behind our behavior, but rather what they really meant was, *"Change your behavior to the way I want you to act."*

Because the question with a "why" is often perceived as criticism, a person usually responds by either withdrawing, attacking, or rationalizing the behavior in response. The "why" question makes us feel we have to give a "reason" for our behavior. Feeling threatened, we do not feel free to explore or examine the reasons that led to the behavior. "Why" demands a response that may not be evident to the person who is being questioned. "Why" requires people to explain themselves, and, as noted, to come up with *reasons* and to rationalize their behavior. When such questions are posed, individuals may tend to become defensive and to feel pressure to "explain away" their behaviors, without seeking changes. This should not be construed as implying that we should never use "why" questions. It is suggested, however, that effective communicators will be cautious in the use of too many "why" questions with their friends, would-be friends, and others regardless of cultural background.

Open-Ended Questions (3)

An open question encourages people to develop their answers and is more person centered. And, in my opinion, it will not be viewed as "too personal," "improper," or "intrusive" by those culturally different. It conveys your *interest* in the person and is the response to your question. However, as noted, the closed question is structured basically for only a "yes" or "no" response and can usually be answered in a few words. Thus, in my opinion, the "safest," the most appropriate, and the most facilitative choice is the open-ended one, especially with someone culturally different. Now, consider the closed questions presented previously and the alternative open-ended question:

"Do you like Lionel a lot?" (closed)

*"**What** is it about Lionel that you find appealing?"* (open)

"Did you like reading that section?" (closed)

*"**How** did you feel about that section?"* (open)

"Are you ready for the test?" (closed)

*"**What** can we do to get you ready for the test?"* (open)

"Do you get along with your parents?" (closed)

*"**What** can you tell me about your relationship with your parents?"* (open)

What do you notice about the open questions? It is my opinion that they show much more *interest* in the other person and basically, seek opinions only. They do not "pry" or "probe." And, we all enjoy someone being interested in us, especially our opinions. Consider this question to you concerning this book: "Do you like my book to this point?" This is a closed question and you'll probably answer with a "yes" or a "no." A better question might be: "What do you like or not like about my book to this point?" Notice the difference? The latter shows more *interest* in your response, is more *inviting,* and is definitely more facilitative.

　　　　　　　　　　　　　　Joe Wittmer, Ph.D.

"How?" and "what?" are useful questions that can lead to deeper understanding. If I ask "how?" I am asking about the quality and process of what is occurring now, instead of leaving the present and guessing about the past. "Why do atoms react the way they do?" is a question for metaphysics, and there are a million useless answers. "How do atoms react?" is a question for physics and chemistry and there is only one very useful answer for each specific situation. "Why do you feel bad?" is at best a request for explanation and justification, and at worst a demand that you deny the fact that you feel bad if you can't justify it. "How do you feel bad?" or "What do you experience?" are real requests for information about your experience, and you answer "I feel tense in my stomach and my head aches," brings you into closer contact with your own experience. Your answer is a real communication that tells me more about yourself. When you ask "how" and "what" you request information about facts and processes. When you ask "why" you ask for endless explanation— the cause of the cause of the cause of the cause of the cause.

John O. Stevens

Certain types of open-ended comments can also be facilitative and invite people to share; i.e., "Oh, I find that interesting. . ." or, "I'd like to know more about that," or "Tell me more about...."

The open question and/or open comment "invites" persons to respond from their own perceptual fields. Again, let us consider two closed questions given previously and some possible open-ended alternatives:

"You don't like college, do you?" (closed)

*"**What** is it about college that you don't like?"* (open)

"Is this the part that's upsetting you?" (closed)

*"**What** part is upsetting you?"* (open)

Of all questions, open-ended questions which begin with *what, how, where,* or *when* are the most facilitative in our conversations with others regardless of their similarity or difference from us. Closed questions may be helpful to gain specific information to clarify a situation, but open questions give people the most room to discover and convey their innermost feelings, ideas, and thoughts about a matter. Open questions are the most person centered because they keep the questioner from getting ahead of the respondent. Open-ended questions enable us to follow another's thinking, rather than have them follow ours.

Individual Practice Activity

In order to help you understand better the difference between open and closed questions, please complete the following worksheet and be prepared to discuss your responses with others in your class or group.

Here are some typical statements from people, followed by closed questions. Read each closed question that follows and then substitute your open question for all three examples. Try to begin each response with *what, how, when* or *where*.

Example 1

Siupo: *Maybe if I had worked harder at Algebra last year, I could have been in Calculus this year.*

Mary: *Are you going to try for it this year?* (closed)

Your open-ended question: _____

_____

Example 2

Ellen: *I can't stand the way Bill treats me.*

Delroy: *Are you going to tell him?* (closed)

Your open-ended question: _____

_____

Example 3

Jose: *I don't think Anglos really want to understand Hispanics.*

Tom: *Are you going to do something about that?* (closed)

Your open-ended question: _____

_____

Group Practice Activity

Instructor's Note:

Using a demonstration group of five or six, ask one person to tell about an actual experience at home, school, work, or play relating to a culturally different person. In a "go-around," have each of the other group members first ask a "why" question (the person being questioned should not answer the questions). Then, in a second go-around, have group members ask open questions (what, how, when, or where). Then, ask the person who received the questions to tell what feelings were experienced when the different questions were asked; "why" Vs. "open-ended." Repeat this procedure with a second person.

In a second demonstration group of five or six, again have someone tell something that happened at home, school, work, or play involving someone culturally different. In a go-around, have the other group members first ask "why" questions of the talker and then, in the second go-around, change their "why" question to either (only) a "what" or a "how" question. Again, the person being questioned should not respond to the individual "why," "what," or "how" questions. Then, again, ask the person being questioned to tell what was experienced when the different questions were asked. This procedure might also be repeated with a third person, perhaps using a different topic.

Group Practice Activity

Instructor's Note:

Divide the class/group members into triads. Have individuals in each of the triads number themselves 1, 2, and 3. Number 1 begins by telling something "You do to have fun." Number 2 asks any two questions about the topic to which number 1 responds. Number 3 then tells what types of questions (i.e., why, open or closed, and so forth) were asked.

Then, the procedures are repeated with each of the other two triad members having the opportunity to be the talker (i.e., serve the role of number 1 above).

Outside Assignment

Keep a record of how many "why" questions and closed questions you ask and receive over the next 24 hours. Then, in the following 24 hours, make a deliberate attempt not to ask "why" or "closed" questions of anyone. Instead, try to begin each question with *what, how, when,* or *where.* Be prepared to discuss your feelings about this exercise during the next meeting of your group or class.

Outside Assignment

Keep a record of how often you receive *untimely advice* or *evaluation* and how often your behavior is *interpreted* by others during the next 24 hours. Also, keep a record of the number of times you make these responses to others.

Clarifying and Summarizing (2)

Any response that indicates your attempt to understand accurately what a person has said, or to identify the most significant ideas emerging from what was said, is termed a clarification or summary statement. Such a statement, a "repeat," "rephrasing," or "reformulating" a person's "story" or "message," is helpful when there is some doubt as to whether you are really "with" the other person's thinking and feeling. Clarification or summary statements are used to help individuals feel that you have "heard" and are attempting to understand the content of what they have just said.

The greatest compliment that was ever paid to me was when one asked me what I thought, and attended to my answer.

Henry David Thoreau

When there is a lot of talk in a spontaneous, fast conversation, a person cannot expect to understand everything. A timely attempt to let another know that we are interested in following his or her thoughts and what is being said can help facilitate communication. As noted, a clarification statement involves "fresh" (or new) words in an attempt to restate (or repeat) that which has just been stated. However, you do not get "credit" for a clarification statement or summary unless you use it *timely,* use words *other than those used by the talker,* and keep the statement *short* and *to the point* just made by the talker. Clarification also is an attempt to simplify or focus what has been said. Clarification or summary statements focus primarily on *ideas* or *content* of the discussion. This emphasis separates these responses from those described in the next section (tuning in to feelings responses). Clarification and summary statements also provide "wiggle room" for subsequent responses. They can help you to "recover," when perhaps of ignorance of one's cultural values, or whatever, you have "goofed" during an interpersonal encounter. Used genuinely, such a response lets a person know that you seek further clarification. Consider the following:

"If I hear you correctly, you are telling me that...."

"You seem to be saying that...."

"If I am following you, you're saying...."

"Correct me if I'm wrong, but you're thinking...."

"Let me see if I understand what you are saying; you said...."

"So, in other words...."

"Let's see, your aim is to...."

"What I hear emerging from what you've said is...."

Clarifying and summary responses are not meant to be used in *all* of our conversations with others. They are for people interested in facilitative communication, when they want to check out (when appropriate) the other person's thoughts or ideas. As noted, such statements reassure people they are being listened to. Such statements reveal to the speaker that they've been "heard"—a process of active instead of passive listening. Other examples include:

"It appears you're telling me that this...."

"Let me see now, you're saying that...."

"Let's see, you said... and... and...."

Consider an 18-year-old female college freshman who complains to her roommate about the way she has to get to school. She says, with much emotion, "I hate to ride the city bus! I have to get up so early and then wait and wait for the dumb bus! I'm going to ask my parents to buy me a car to drive, or at least a moped. Just about anything would be better than riding the dumb old bus!" Any one of the following might have been said to her by the roommate:

1. "You should think about your parents. Its not easy for them to send you to college. You should get a job and buy your own car." *(Advising and Evaluating:* Ignores the person's ideas and feelings and puts the focus on her parents.)

2. "I can remember when I used to ride the bus. It was a good time to study." *(Reassuring and Supporting:* An attempt to support, but it draws attention away from the person's own experiences and feelings.)

3. "If you didn't ride the bus, you'd have a hard time getting to school, wouldn't you? You would have to walk and that wouldn't be any fun then, would it?" (A *closed question:* Presumptuous, closed questions leave no room for the person to expand on ideas and feelings.)

A person who wants to facilitate the conversation, to make it easier for the respondent to answer, however, might have said any one of the following:

1. "Riding the bus is really no fun for you." *(Clarifying and Summarizing:* An attempt to clarify a central theme of the person's words. Does not imply why it isn't fun (which would be an interpretation).

2. "You're hoping your parents will buy you a vehicle to drive to school." *(Clarifying and Summarizing:* Ignores feelings, but generally clarifies the person's words in a short statement. Shows being "with" the person, without judgment.)

3. "It seems to me from what you've said that riding the bus gets your day off to a bad start at school." *(Clarifying and Summarizing:* Attempts to get at feelings, but gets into drawing the conclusion that school is unpleasant. The qualifying phrase (It seems to me..., however, gives the person some "wiggle room.")

The next time you watch a television talk show, notice how often the host or hostess makes clarifying or summarizing type statements. It puts the guest at ease and communication flows easily. Also, you will hear effective sales people use this response often. But again, both the effective talk show host and salesperson use such responses in an *appropriate* and *timely* fashion.

Clarifying and summarizing responses usually are more difficult to learn and use because they are not heard very often. A word of caution: *do not overuse such a response.* As noted, like advice, they too must be used in a timely fashion. That is, if someone were to ask you what day it is, you would not respond with clarification, you would answer them directly!

To give an untimely summary or clarifying response, even to a best friend, sounds trite to the talker. Be *genuine* in your use of this response. Use it when you want to be "with" the person, to put a "chip in the bank," or when you actually want to understand better what has just been said. To use such a response too often, especially in an untimely manner, may "drive your friends up the wall," and you may be accused of "playing counselor."

As previously indicated (in Chapter I), facilitative type responses such as clarification/summary are rarely used in *informal* relationships (a neighbor whom you really do not know, and so forth) or in *impersonal structured relationships* (with the mail carrier, the shoe salesperson, and so forth). This response is best reserved for use in your *personal* relationships (friends, would-be friends, work associates, colleagues, others you know well or hope to know well).

Individual Practice Activity

Read the statements following and write your clarifying or summarizing responses to each; a "repeat," a "re-phrasing", a "clarification," or a "summary." Keep it short and use words other than those used by the talker.

Example 1

Tamara: *I'm sure having trouble living with my Asian American roommate. He's so shy and he seldom says anything.*

Your clarification response: _____

_____

Example 2

Marianne: *Blacks often view Asian Americans as the group getting all the breaks.*

Your clarification response: _____

_____

Example 3

Linda: *I just moved here from Michigan a year ago, and I really miss the cold weather.*

Your clarification response: _____

_____

Example 4

Wong: *In my culture, families like mine are real close and I really miss mine.*

Your clarification response: _____

_____

Again, be prepared to discuss your responses with your group or class.

Group Practice Activity

Instructor's Note:

Form a demonstration group of five or six people. Give each group a magic marker (or pencil). Have one person volunteer to tell something that has happened recently at work or school concerning a member of a culturally different group. Without identifying anyone in advance, the magic marker is passed by the talker to someone in the group (not as a go-around procedure) who then *clarifies* or *summarizes* what was said and follows it by then asking the speaker an *open* question (what, how, when or where) to learn (a little) more about the situation, i.e., "So, its as if this happens often. *How* do you respond to him when he says that?" After hearing the speaker's response, the marker holder passes it to someone else who *clarifies* or *summarizes* before asking the speaker an *open* question. The speaker responds one more time. This marker holder passes the marker to someone else who makes a final *clarifying* or *summarizing* response, followed by an open question, before becoming the new speaker. This procedure is repeated for each member of the group.

Outside Assignment

Interview another person (someone not in your group) about a time in life when that person stood up for someone of a different culture, race, or religion. Try to use only open-ended questions or clarifying/summarizing statements during your interview. Type out a 3-minute segment of your interview (the other's statements and your responses). Bring your typescript to the next meeting and be prepared to discuss it with your small group.

Tuning In to Feelings

The way you *feel* at this moment determines to a great extent how you *perceive* and *feel* about the words you are now reading (this book). This perception determines, to a great extent, how you will *behave* toward what you are reading and the associated activities found at the end of this chapter. That is, if you had a bad night and are feeling depressed or down, you probably see these words in a negative manner, i.e., "I hate these types of things!" and you behave accordingly (slumped, arms folded across your chest, frowning). However, if you are feeling good, pleased, or happy, you probably view things differently, with positive anticipation and even some excitement ("Maybe I can learn something from this.") As we *feel*, so we *perceive*, so we *behave*. The clarification summary response discussed previously is aimed more at the talker's perception while the tuning in to responses go back to—are sensitive to—the feeling(s) of the talker.

Our feelings are our sixth sense, the sense that interprets, arranges, directs and summarizes the other five. Feelings tell us whether what we experience is threatening, painful, regretful, sad or joyous.... More than anything else feelings make us human.

P. Viscott

An individual's *perception is* his or her *reality* (i.e., the way we see and behave toward the world and others) at that moment— I see, I feel, I do! Thus, if we want to understand another person, we begin by understanding that person's feelings and/or perceptions without judgment or evaluation. We do this by being sensitive to that person's behavior (be it verbal or non-verbal) and by making facilitative statements that go behind the behavior to the perceptions and feelings causing or proceeding the specific behavior. That is, we make timely and appropriate non-judgmental statements that show that we are tuning in to feelings and/or perceptions with understanding. We (temporarily) "walk in another's shoes" without judgment. Again, this is a response that *must* be used in a timely fashion and most probably, in *personal* type relationships only. And, it should be acknowledged that certain cultural groups may be more hesitant to share feelings than others. For example, Sue and Sue (1990), as well as Fukuyama and Cox-Inoue (Chapter 6), indicated that Asian Americans may experience difficulty when asked to deal directly with their feelings. However, it is my opinion that a tuning in to feelings response is *not* requesting or even suggesting that a feeling be expressed. It is simply making a statement indicating that we are *attempting* to *understand* or to be tuned in to the feelings of the talker. As noted, a person cannot not reveal feelings. It is my opinion that when a person's feelings (regardless of cultural background) are understood in a *timely* and *appropriate* manner, the interpersonal relationship will be enhanced and communication made easier. However, if such a response causes embarrassment to the individual, "recover" by apologizing in an authentic manner, and genuinely request clarification.

Do we all think, perceive, and feel alike? This controversy has been argued by anthropologists and psychologists for decades. And, it is my belief that feelings and thoughts are greatly influenced by culture. That is, we do not all see things the same way; the way we see and feel about things is *dependent on our cultural background.* Thus, it seems important that we make every possible attempt, when appropriate and timely, to tune in to the feelings of those friends, associates, and so forth, different from us so that better communication is facilitated.

Torrey (1986) indicated that cultural variation in perception and thinking has been substantiated by research. For example, he cited research indicating that the Hanunoo, a group of people found in the Philippines, divide all colors into four—mabiru, malagiti, marara, and malatuy—i.e., marara includes red, orange, yellow, and maroon. Thus, if you were to show a Hanunoo a piece of cloth that is red, orange, and yellow (our colors) that person would say it is "marara." Torrey further stated that the Dani people of New Guinea do not count beyond two. This is not because of a lack of intelligence. They simply divide up their world differently than we do—one, two, and many! These may be extreme examples of cultural variation in perception and thinking, but, as stated, tuning in to the feelings of someone different from us (without a value judgment) during an interpersonal encounter may be one of the most facilitative responses we can make. This response conveys to others that we are "reading" (or attempting to read) how they are feeling. It communicates that we are trying to know how they are experiencing their world at the moment—their "here" and "now" experience. For example:

*"You seem **angry**, Harold."*

*"That's **confusing** to you."*

*"You're **tired**."*

Notice that we do not go on to tell them *why* they feel a certain way. Adding the "why," the "reason" or the "because" behind the feeling would be an interpretation/analysis type response.

The tuning in to feeling response can be (but need not be) difficult to learn because it demands that we be empathic listeners. It requires that we listen beyond mere words to the *feelings* being communicated, to *reflect*—to *restate* (using our own words)—these feelings back to the person. When used appropriately, reflection of feelings responses put (big) "chips in the bank" with the other person. It brings you closer as individuals regardless of your respective culture.

We pay a high price when we've:
*   looked without seeing*
*   listened without hearing*
*   spoken without meaning*
*   moved without awareness*
*   touched without feeling.*

The price is in not feeling good about ourselves and others, not feeling loved, not getting things done, and not having hope.

Virginia Satir

As noted, this type of statement should not be confused with clarification, which tends to re-emphasize the *content* behind what is being expressed. Neither should it be confused with interpretation, which tends to explain *why* a person feels a certain way. Rather, it focuses upon the feeling the other person is conveying as sensed by the facilitator at the moment. However, understand that to begin a sentence with "you feel" is not necessarily reflecting feeling. For example, "I feel that you would make a good athlete" is not a feeling oriented response. It is an opinion. To make a feeling response, we must go beyond the mere words to get to the feeling. Sometimes it can be helpful to ask yourself, "How would I feel to have said that?" Or, "How would I have to feel to do something like that?" And then ask yourself, "If I felt that way, how would I behave?"

After making feeling focused responses timely and effectively, we have insight into that person's feelings. If our insights are accurate and compatible with what we are sensing from the other person, then the feeling is stated correctly. However, remember that we can distort what some people say. Our own value systems and inabilities at times prevent us from being sensitive to another person's feelings, especially if that person is from a different culture.

No one, as noted, regardless of culture, can talk without showing feelings. All of us feel something at all times, and both verbal and nonverbal cues tell us how a person feels. Feelings can be categorized into: (a) pleasant feelings or (b) unpleasant feelings. Sometimes a person will convey both *pleasant* and *unpleasant* feelings in the same statement, i.e., "Our ski trip was really great the first day and then the next day I took a bad spill and broke my leg," i.e., both a *pleasant* (excitement) and an *unpleasant* feeling (disappointment) were expressed. Thus, when listening to a person talk, we should ask ourselves: Do I hear unpleasant feelings, pleasant feelings, or both being expressed? Think about the feeling words that might best describe what is heard or sensed from the other person. If we hear pleasant feelings, we might say:

*"You're **excited**."*

*"You talk about your culture with a lot of **pride**."*

*"You seem so **delighted** with the idea."*

*"You're really **pleased** with yourself."*

*"I sense a real feeling of **dedication** toward them."*

*"The whole thing **fascinated** you."*

On the other hand, if we hear unpleasantness, we might say:

*"It was a **painful** experience for you."*

*"You're really **angry**."*

*"I hear **confusion** when you talk about how your people have been treated."*

*"You're **discouraged** and wonder what's the use."*

*"I sense a lot of **sadness** when you speak of your friends still in Vietnam."*

*"It can be so **irritating** to you."*

Maybe we hear both pleasant and unpleasant feelings, or ambivalence, in which case we might say:

*"It's **challenging** to you, but you feel **awkward** just starting."*

*"The first experience with your African American colleague **disappointed** you, but you're **encouraged** now about new possibilities."*

*"You're **excited** about going to college, but **afraid** you might not be as good a student as people say you are."*

*"You were feeling so **optimistic** and then suddenly things looked **gloomy**."*

*"You're feeling **loved**, yet **shut-in**."*

*"You're **interested**, but feeling **cautious**, too."*

In the example presented previously of the college student who "hated" to ride the bus, the facilitative roommate might have used the tuning in to feeling response to say:

*"It really **annoys** you at times to ride the bus."* (Gets to the basic feeling.)

*"Riding the bus isn't much **fun** for you."* (Captures the feeling tone and mirrors back the person's overall picture being presented.)

*"Waiting for the bus can really be **tiring**."* (Attends to a present feeling and gives it selective attention.)

> *If we take people as they are, we make them worse. If we treat them as if they were what they ought to be, we help them to become what they are capable of becoming.*
>
> *Goethe*

After responding to feelings, the facilitative individual does not "rush on" with other statements unless appropriate at that instant. A facilitator lets the response and its impact take full effect. More often than not, if you are reasonably accurate in making such responses, the person will unconsciously nod, as if to say "Yes, thanks for listening," and talk some more because you have been "facilitative." Pause a little after you give such a response to give the person opportunity to experience your interest and understanding. As one of my students said, "Let it soak." It is a pleasant experience for both speaker and listener. However, making a suggestion to the person, or asking an open question when seeking more information, immediately following a tuning in to feeling response is also highly facilitative.

It should be noted that when we respond to a person's feelings, our statements can be rejected. Some individuals have difficulty acknowledging their feelings, and may even deny them. And, as noted, this may be more prevalent in some cultures than others. However, it is important that the response be made in our *personal* relationships because it communicates that we are *trying* or attempting to understand the person. Appropriate and timely tuning in to responses communicate, "I'm not only listening to your words, but also to that special part of you behind the words." The statement is "facilitative" regardless of whether it is acknowledged as such, and later the person may recognize and express appreciation for the accurate reflection. Attempting to understand (even if we miss) still puts a "chip in the bank" with that person! And, even if you "miss," that person will most likely fill you in, i.e., "No, it's not the pain of the whole thing, it's...."

Few people have experienced individuals in their lives who really sensed their whole being, and responded with accurate understanding. The white Anglo culture has not actively encouraged the disclosure of feelings, especially among males. Feelings too often are viewed as private, and only are allowed to "come out after dark." Even then, however, many believe the "proper" thing to do is to disown, deny, or distort them for fear that they will reveal a character weakness. Consequently, distant and formal interpersonal relationships that lack personal understanding have been the norm in our society. Fortunately, however, this situation is changing, and in positive directions.

We are learning that "hiding" feelings can be a step to emotional discomfort and disturbance. Our society's patterns of interpersonal communication have fostered far too much mental illness, dehumanized relationships, and too many dysfunctional individuals. Facilitative people accept part of the responsibility for reversing the factors which have impeded positive personal growth in others, especially with those who are culturally different.

Intentionally tuning in to feelings traditionally has been used by counselors and therapists. Recently, however, there has been considerable interest in teaching this skill, along with the other facilitative communication skills, to a variety of people in a variety of situations. Parents, employers, employees, salespeople, supervisors, students, administrators, children, and teachers are among the many finding feeling-focused responses helpful. They are becoming "everyday facilitators." However, we have a long way to go before facilitative responding is ingrained in our society, especially between different cultures, races, and religions.

Regardless of the advantages, or facilitative value, a tuning in to feelings statement is not appropriate in *all* or even most situations. And, it may be a response that you use only sparingly. Sometimes people simply are seeking information, not trying to work out their feelings. At such times mirroring back a feeling is out of place, inappropriate, and untimely. If someone asks you for the time of day, you would do better simply to give the information than to respond by saying, "You're *concerned* about the time of day." If you're fixing dinner and someone wants to know when it will be ready, it would be exasperating to hear, "You're *interested* in knowing when we'll be eating." Those are "games" that facilitative communicators refuse to play.

However, people often do hide important feelings behind innocent-sounding statements. In such cases, mirroring brings their real concern into the open. But do not go overboard with the technique. Usually, if there is a feeling hidden behind a statement, you will recognize some accompanying nonverbal clue such as a change in facial expression, tone of voice, posture, and so on. It takes attention, concentration, and caring on your part to spot the times when reflecting/mirroring responses are appropriate and timely.

Some communication researchers have indicated that the success of tuning in to another person's feelings depends on the attitude we bring to the interpersonal situation. Too often we think of reflecting of feelings as a kind of "gimmick" we can use when an unpleasant situation arises. According to these writers, if you think about the technique this way, it is almost sure to fail. In fact, unless you truly mean what you say, you will come across as manipulative, phony, and uncaring. They suggest that as you practice tuning in to others' feelings try and keep the following points in mind:

1. *Do not* tune in to and reflect a feeling unless you truly and sincerely wish to *hear* and *assist* that person. You will be doing both yourself and the other person a disservice if you pretend to care when you really do not.

2. *Do not* tune in to and reflect a feeling if you are not willing to take the necessary time to truly tune in, listen, and to continue the conversation. If you are willing to make the effort, you will probably be rewarded. But you will only lose the speaker's trust if you commit yourself and then do not follow through.

3. You have the right to *expose* but not to *impose* your ideas or values on the other person. Tuning in means accepting other people's feelings and trusting that they can find their own solutions. You serve as a catalyst. Your efforts to moralize, or to change the speaker might be helpful, but if you decide to use this approach, do so honestly—do not mask it in the guise of pretending to care.

4. Keep your attention focused on the person speaking. Sometimes it is easy to become defensive, relate their thoughts to your own life, or seek further information just to satisfy your own curiosity as you listen to others share feelings. Do not become a "feeling voyeur." Remember, tuning in to and reflecting a feeling is a form of communication with someone else at a *deeper* level. Keep your energy focused on this goal. (Adler, Rosenfeld & Towne, 1989).

One final example will, perhaps, assist to better explain the communication model presented in this chapter:

Assume that your spouse, significant other, your roommate, or someone else with whom you are rather *close* comes home from work and adamantly states: "I had the worst day of my life! The boss jumped all over me for no reason and I'm sick and tired of that lousy job!" How might you respond? What would be your first response? A non-facilitative response might be: "You think you had a bad day! You should have been with me, I...." Or, maybe an *untimely* advice/evaluation type statement: "You're taking that job too seriously, what you need to do is...." (7). Or, perhaps an untimely interpretation/analysis response: "I know why you had a bad day, you stayed up too late watching TV last night." (6). Or maybe an *inappropriate* support/reassurance response: "Things are going to be better tomorrow. Put your feet up and...." (5). Or we might ask a non-facilitative question: "Why did you let him get to you like that?" Or, "Did you tell him off?" (Closed) (4). A more facilitative question might be: "What happened that made your day so bad?" (3) Or, a clarification/summary (2) response might have been very appropriate: "It was a long, tough day for you," maybe followed by, "I'm sorry," or perhaps another open-ended question. This appears to have been a good, appropriate time to tune in to the feelings (1) of the talker with a simple, "Work today was really frustrating"—and let it "soak" for a moment before saying anything additional. Most likely your "accurate empathy" will bring a response like, "Yes, it really was, I...."

As noted, each of us has a unique perceptual field. True communication with another, therefore, is the merging of two perceptual fields. The two perceptual fields (circles) *must* overlap if two-way communication is to occur. Overlap in perceptual fields results in mutual understanding, positive identification, and empathy with one another. Misunderstanding and miscommunication result from a failure of individuals to find perceptual commonality. Such overlap of perceptions, and resulting open communication, cannot occur if individuals are defensive with one another. Untimely advice, judgment, and interpretation add to such miscommunication while open-ended questions, timely and appropriate clarification/summary, and tuning in to feelings responses bring about more trusting and open relationships.

We think of communication as primarily the "words" we use. Words do help to transmit meanings, and the ability to use words well makes us effective communicators. Remember, however, that nonverbal communication also plays an important role in interpersonal relationships and that we can also tune in to the feelings behind a person's nonverbal behavior.

By now you can see that the tuning in to feelings response requires a combination of interest, determination, and skill. However, by responding effectively with reflection/mirroring, you can learn more about others, help others, and promote your interpersonal relationships with them at the same time.

References

Sue, D.W. & Sue, D. (1990). *Counseling the culturally different: Theory and practice.* New York: John Wiley.

Torrey, E.F. (1986). *Witchdoctors and psychiatrists,* Northvale, NJ: Jason Aronson.

Individual Practice Activity

The following exercises are provided to help you develop further your skills in the tuning in to feeling responses. Be prepared to discuss your responses with your group or class.

Example 1:

Fellow Student: *You know, Eldon really ticks me off with that condescending attitude of his!*

Your tuning in to feelings response: _____

_____

Example 2:

Fellow Student: *Maybe if I had worked harder at understanding Blacks, I wouldn't be in this jam now.*

Your tuning in to feelings response: _____

_____

Example 3:

Parent: *Sometimes I just don't understand your friend Denise, especially when I know that she gets along great with all of the African American kids in the dorm.*

Your tuning in to feelings response: _____

_____

Example 4:

Friend: *It would really be great to go to the beach with you guys, but I just couldn't stand the notion of not studying some more for that Monday exam.*

Your tuning in to feelings response: _____

_____

Group Practice Activity

Instructor's Note:

Form a demonstration group of 5 or 6 people. Place them in a semi-circle in front of the large group, or perhaps in the center of the group (as an inside circle, the "fishbowl" technique). Ask the others (outside the demonstration group) to watch and listen. Have the demonstration group think of words that describe *pleasant* feelings. As the group members say different words, write them down. Add others as they are offered.

Remind the group that a feeling word vocabulary is important if we are to respond to feelings. Most of us need to get beyond our "second grade feeling vocabulary" — happy, mad, glad, sad, good, and bad. Then, ask someone in the demonstration group to tell about something that happened during the week. After the person talks (briefly) about an event (interrupt at a convenient point, if necessary, or ask the person to say a little more if it is too brief). Use a go-around procedure for the group to, in turn, tell if they heard a *pleasant* or an *unpleasant* feeling, or *both*? Then, in a second go-around, have them tell the feeling word(s) they heard, and to re-label the *pleasant* or *unpleasant* or *both* feelings they are aware of in the talker. The group members should focus on feeling words rather than the person's story or situation. That is, focus on the *person* instead of the *event!*

Next, form a second demonstration group and repeat the procedure. Then, have a second person in the group tell something that happened during the week, something with someone from a different culture, if possible. Now, however, have the group members do the first step (i.e., identify if *pleasant, unpleasant* feelings or *both* are being communicated) silently to themselves. Next, use a go-around procedure in which each member

_____

says an appropriate feeling word aloud. Finally, ask the person who shared the event how close the group seems to be in tuning into his or her feelings.

In the next phase, a third person in the same demonstration group tells something. This time, however, the first two steps are conducted silently in each group member's mind (first, pleasant or unpleasant feelings, and then a feeling word or words). Next, in a go-around, group members put their words into a short sentence. Each speaks directly to the person (e.g., James, you felt ____, or, You were feeling ____, or, You were ____, or, It was ____, or, To you ____.)

Participants should not project their own feelings on to others. Our personal projections--how we would feel in the situation--might give us some leads, but they should be checked carefully with what is actually being experienced by the person.

Joe Wittmer, Ph.D.

Group Practice Activity

Instructor's Note:

The purpose of this activity is to provide participants with the opportunity to learn and practice the more facilitative responses (i.e., clarifying and summarizing, tuning in to and understanding of feelings, and open-ended questions). It also increases two-way communication and can increase self-disclosure.

First, form the members of the group/class into triads. Have triad members number themselves 1, 2, and 3. Let 1 be the talker, 2 the facilitator, and 3 the observer. Mix triads by gender and race if possible. Next, the talker (being real; not role playing) speaks to the facilitator for three minutes about his or her negative feelings regarding *"A past incident with a culturally different individual,"* or, *"What personal characteristics prevent you from being a better communicator with those different from you?"* Choose one.

The facilitator should assist the talker (without approval or disapproval) in speaking about him or herself. The facilitator should attempt to reflect (mirror) in "fresh" words the ideas and feelings the talker is expressing. Remember, during the next three minutes there should be *no advice, reassurance, closed-questions, or interpretation!* Facilitators should use sensitivity and let the talker know that the facilitator is trying to understand. (It should be acknowledged that this is *not* the way we respond to others in everyday situations—this is over-learning, over-practicing these skills.)

During the three minutes the observer in each group watches the facilitator and records his or her observations by marking on *The Facilitator's Checklist* which follows.

The Facilitator's Check List

HE/SHE	YES	NO
1. Interpreted or analyzed	❏	❏
2. Evaluated or gave untimely advice	❏	❏
3. Responded empathically	❏	❏
4. Listened well	❏	❏
5. Inappropriately supported and/or reassured	❏	❏
6. Interrupted unnecessarily	❏	❏
7. Attempted to reflect ideas and feelings using fresh words	❏	❏
8. Seemed sensitive to what the talker was saying	❏	❏
9. Facilitated the talker to continue talking	❏	❏
10. Denied or avoided obvious feelings of the talker	❏	❏

After about three minutes, the observer, using the check list, feeds back the observations to the facilitator/listener for about two minutes (peer learning). The observer should tell the facilitator about what was seen and heard. Was the facilitator sensitive? Was he or she a good listener? Did the facilitator have good eye contact? Did he or she *reflect* and *clarify* without giving approval or disapproval?

Next, give the talker (same person) a new assignment (again, no role playing). The talker should speak for about three minutes on the *positive aspects of becoming a better communicator with the culturally different.* Or, talk about a pleasant experience with someone different. The assignments for the other two members of the triad also should remain the same.

Next, switch roles in a second and third round (with each triad member taking one of the previous roles) until all three have taken each part. It is suggested that the *same* talking assignments, first negative and then positive, be given to everyone when it is time to talk. Watch as the groups become closer as they realize that, in the absence of advice, interpretation, and so forth, it is easy to become trusting of others.

Joe Wittmer, Ph.D.

Group Practice Activity

Pick Your Corner

This activity will stimulate communication on important issues, force clarification of positions, and increase understanding of other's points of view.

Instructor's Note:

Designate one corner of the room as the *"Strongly Disagree"* section, another as the *"Strongly Agree"* section, a third as the *"Disagree"* section, and a fourth as *"Agree"* section. The center of the room might be designated as *"Uncertain."* Then, ask all participants to stand. Next, make a statement such as: *"Minorities are getting too many breaks in America today;"* or *"We should push segregation not integration;" "Marijuana should be legalized;" "Affirmative Action is not working;"* or *"Regardless of culture, we're all more similar than different."* Give the participants time to think about the options in the different "corners" of the room. Then, request that each *walk* to the corner that best matches their personal opinions/feelings about the statement. "Go where your heart tells you to go, not to where your friends go!"

Allow time for the participants (maybe in groups of five) in each corner to discuss among themselves their reasons for choosing the particular corner. They might even make a list of reasons that led them to be there. Then, hold a general discussion as members listen to the statements from each of the different corners. You might bring a few from various groups into a "fishbowl" circle, perhaps to debate the issue or to try and convince the "Uncertain" group to pick a corner.

Later, you might reassemble the entire class/group, read the statement again and ask the participants to go to the corner their parents (teachers, African Americans, or others) might choose. Again, allow time for discussion among those who select a particular corner. Request that the *high facilitative responses be used.*

Group Practice Activity

Communication Between the Races/Cultures

This is an exercise aimed at facilitating communication between two different races or cultures and to heighten awareness of stereotypes/prejudices, and so forth.

Instructor's Note:

From among all the class/group members, form two circles, one circle within another, i.e., Blacks might sit in the inside circle while all non-Blacks sit on the outside. For the first ten minutes encourage the Blacks to talk about communication problems with Anglos (in general), venting their unpleasant and pleasant feelings (no personal names). The outer circle of non-Blacks observes but does not participate in the discussion. After about ten minutes, the circles are reversed, with the non-Blacks on the inside responding to the same task (problems in communication with Blacks, in general).

Next, have both groups together discuss how they felt about the activity and what they learned from it. Additional questions to each group might be posed by group members or you. Facilitative responses should be used.

A Variation:

Have females sit in the inside circle and pretend they are males. They talk about how it feels to be "male" and what they like and dislike about it. They might also talk about how they see females, or talk about "Things I like and dislike about being a man or woman," or "Things that I would like to change in our society in terms of being masculine or feminine." Each group might be encouraged to talk about the biggest problem of the opposite sex.

The males write statements about what it feels like to be a male and some of their likes and dislikes. The statements are then given to the circle of females, who read them and respond. For example, "My girlfriend makes me feel cheap when I can't afford to take her to certain places;" or, "Why do guys always have to be the ones to set up a date?" or, "I like a girl, but she doesn't like me," and so forth.

Group Practice Activity

Dear Abby and the Cool Seat

This exercise permits a greater awareness of the problems that those "different" from us are experiencing and provides the opportunity to give timely advice when *preceded* by a tuning in to feelings response.

Instructor's Note:

Place participants in small, culturally homogeneous groups (4 or 5), and ask them to write *Dear Abby* about current problems they are facing relating to their respective racial or cultural backgrounds. Request that they keep the problem statements short (6 or 7 lines) and that they not personally refer to anyone.

The *Dear Abby* procedure is a fish bowl type discussion activity to be used with large groups. After the problems are written (they might also be written by individual participants), develop a horseshoe-type circle up front with the opening toward the larger group, and call for 6 volunteers, i.e., six Anglos, three males and three females, to enter into the "fish bowl" and to play the part of *Dear Abby*—to give "timely advice" to the i.e., African American, Asian American, Hispanic American, and other participants who have written *Dear Abby*. That is, they are to solve the participants' problems *written by those different from them*. The horseshoe shape permits an empty chair at its opening which is termed the *"cool seat"* and is so designated by a large, printed sign on the back of the chair. Fishbowl members (i.e., the six Anglos) are in the *"hotseats"* at this time. Any member from the audience (not in the fish bowl) may join the fishbowl only by standing behind the "cool seat" chair. You, or someone of your choice, should serve as facilitator in the fishbowl and begin the process by giving one of the Anglo participants a problem, ie., a Hispanic participant wrote to *Dear Abby*, who, in turn, as *Dear Abby* solves the Hispanic participant's problems. However, the person playing *Dear Abby* should always state the feeling(s) they think the writer is *feeling* (pleasant, unpleasant or both) to have written such a statement prior to giving the timely advice. Then, they indicate how a person who is feeling that way usually *behaves*. That is, prior to giving timely advice to the writer of the problem, members in the "hotseats" are asked to *tune in to* the feelings of each writer and indicate what actions such feelings usually cause—"What would the writer most likely be feeling?" Then, "What behavior(s) would such a feeling most likely cause?" Then they follow with timely advice.

This almost always creates a lively discussion and many people from the outside group may line up behind the cool seat to voice their views. However, they get only 30 seconds in the "cool seat" and are requested not to use personal names, to stay with the topic, and so forth. After the Anglo "hotseat," participants solve the Hispanic participant's problems (about one half hour), call up 6 Hispanic volunteers to enter the fishbowl and to, in turn, solve the problems written to *Dear Abby* by, i.e., Anglo/Black/Asian American participants, and others. Again, advice should be preceded by tuning in to feeling statements followed by a statement concerning the behavior most likely resulting from such feelings. Because of the obvious emotions and tension brought about by this activity, be prepared to facilitate and demonstrate by using the *high facilitative responses.*

A Variation:

Have the males and females write to *Dear Abby* and in turn solve one another's problems, tuning in to feelings, resulting behavior, and so forth, taking turns in the "hotseat."

Outside Activity

The following are some samples of the *Dear Abby* statements written by college students in my undergraduate course on Intercultural Communication. Respond, in writing, to each writer below who is culturally different from you and be prepared to share your responses with others. *Write the "feeling" word and subsequent "behaviors" for each person along with your timely advice for each writer.*

Dear Abby:

I'm a black female and I arrived on campus last Fall. I immediately became interested in pledging a sorority. Some of my black friends tried to talk me out of going through rush but I went anyway. Rush, was great! The sorority girls were very friendly, treated me well and I felt welcome wherever I went. But, disappointment set in quickly. You see, I didn't get a single bid to join! I can't help but think its because I'm Black. I plan to go through rush again next fall. What can I do to assure that I'll be selected this time?

> Signed,
>
> Left Out

Dear Abby:

As an Anglo student I don't understand why we have a Black History Month on campus. Explain to me why special attention is given to this group and not to other groups. It seems very unfair. Why not an Asian History Month? An Anglo History Month? A Hispanic History Month? Please help me to understand this.

> Signed,
>
> Bothered

Dear Abby:

As a White member of a fraternity, racial jokes are commonly told among the brothers. I am against telling such jokes that demean other people but I don't know how to tell them without feeling like they will not understand my concerns. How should I handle this situation?

> Signed,
>
> Alone in a Crowd

Dear Abby:

I'm a White female with a Black roommate who is a very nice person. However, on weekends I tend to socialize with White friends. My roommate sometimes asks what I'll be doing this coming weekend and I always feel uncomfortable and guilty when I say I've already got plans made with friends. Should I invite my roommate to join my activity without asking my other friends? What should I do if my friends say they don't want to invite my roommate?

Signed,

Confused

Dear Abby:

I'm a Cuban American student. I speak Spanish at home but I have lived in the US most of my life so I speak English without an accent. While the color of my skin is black, I consider myself to be Hispanic. Others, both students and faculty, consider me to be Black and classify me as such. It really bothers me that they ignore my real cultural background because of the color of my skin. What can I do to solve this problem?

Signed,

Upset

Dear Abby:

I am an Asian American and believe that I speak English quite well. However, it is obvious to me that other students, and even the faculty, don't think so. They are always asking me to speak more slowly and to repeat myself. I get the feeling that they really don't want to hear me, that they are biased toward me. This is beginning to affect my school work. What can I do to correct this?

Signed,

Frustrated

Chapter *XI*

Using the Facilitative Responses

It is important to learn how and when to appropriately use the more facilitative responses presented in the last chapter if we desire to improve our interpersonal communication skills. Increasing the frequency of the use of these higher level facilitative responses (open-ended comments/questions, clarification/summary, and tuning in to feelings) in our personal relationships will facilitate better, more effective communication regardless of our or others' gender, race, religion, or cultural background. In addition, as noted, decreasing the frequency of using the least facilitative responses given in the last chapter will also improve our communication with others.

As noted, research has shown that when the frequency of the more facilitative responses increases, people are more likely to perceive us as kind, caring, understanding, respectful, accepting, interested, and easy to converse with persons. It is important to note, however, that *genuineness* is not present on this word list. As stated repeatedly throughout this book, genuineness is our being *real,* open, and honest in our relationships. And, also as noted throughout this book, genuineness conveys sincerity, that we are not attempting to fool anyone. When a person is playing a role, i.e., pretending to be a certain way, there is high probability that the "playing" will prevent the person from being a facilitative communicator. And, the more facilitative responses should be used only in a *genuine* manner or not at all.

When people first increase use of the more facilitative responses, especially tuning in to another's feelings and clarifying or summarizing, they often experience awkward moments. High facilitative responses are not common in our interpersonal conversations and they at times feel out-of-place and inappropriate. And, like all verbal responses, they can be given *inappropriately* and in an *untimely* manner. And, as noted, when first beginning to practice these "new" responses, be prepared to feel awkward, or uncomfortable. In addition, you may feel less than genuine because the behavior seems forced and does not flow easily. If practicing, let your friends know that is what you are doing— practicing some new skills! However, remember you need not always be accurate when tuning in to another. The attempt at "understanding" is just as important in establishing and maintaining a facilitative relationship as is always being accurate in your feeling reflection.

Like other new skills, using facilitative responses requires practice to become effective and easy. With practice, they become an integrated part of your personality. Their use then takes less effort and concentration and the responses flow naturally when they become a part of your everyday, interpersonal communication pattern. It should also be acknowledged that decreasing the use of the less facilitative responses, i.e., the "why" question, the "closed" question, "untimely" advice, also take effort, concentration, and practice.

The game of golf provides an excellent analogy. For those of us who have tried the game, or perhaps watched it on television, we know there are many exercises which a professional might use to teach someone to play golf. Professionals might give neophyte golfers the correct grip, and then tell them to keep their eyes on the ball. Beginners are shown how to position their body, move their hips, and hold their hands in the aloft position, and then told, "Remember, let it fly and finish high." It seems like so much to remember! But we know that many, many people learn to play golf. Practice makes perfect (or at least a lot better).

If we observe very closely, we can see several differences in the golf swings of great golfers such as Chi Chi Rodriguez, Nick Faldo, Lee Trevino, Greg Norman, Nancy Lopez, Tom Watson, and Jack Nicklaus. However, all of them are effective and successful golfers. They are beyond the stage of "keep your eye on the ball, keep your left elbow in tight," and all the other little suggestions. They have *integrated* the techniques into their game styles. Because of many hours of practice, they no longer feel awkward in hitting a golf ball; rather, they sense when their swing is correct and when it is not.

While all of them have their own ways of approaching a golf game, just as all facilitative communicators have their own individual styles of responding to another, they all know the basic elements of a good golf stroke, as well as the purpose of the game. All of them know how to use the "tools" available. The "purpose of the game" here is to become a better communicator with those similar and different from us. The "tools" are the more facilitative responses given in the last chapter.

To become a "facilitative" individual, it is important to learn to use high facilitative responses so that they become "spontaneous" reactions. As we practice, we come to sense which "tool" to use, if any, at a specific time. We will know when to tune in to another's feeling, when to clarify the content of the talker, when to show our interest with an open-ended question, and so forth. And, you will learn when not to tune in, and so forth. There will be times when (timely) advice will be the most appropriate response.

The More Facilitative Responses: A Summary

As stated in the preface of this book, you can *improve* your interpersonal communication skills. As also stated several times throughout this book, the facilitative skills presented herein may *not* be appropriately used when conversing with all people in all cultures. In addition, I have stated repeatedly that the more facilitative responses (tuning in to feelings and clarification/ summary of content) should be reserved for use in your "personal" relationships. That is, if you desire to truly listen, to hear, to understand, and/or attempt to understand those similar or different, use these higher level responses timely and appropriately.

The open-ended questions should be used when you desire to invite the talker to continue because you are *genuinely* interested in what is being said. Open-ended questions, those beginning with what, how, when or where, can and should be used in your everyday conversation. However, it is my opinion that no guidelines need be established for their use. That is, open-ended questions can be appropriately used in your personal as well as impersonal relationships.

It is sometimes appropriate to clarify or summarize that which was just said by the other person—the second highest facilitative response presented. That is, if you wish to put "chips in the bank", if you want to assist the person to feel more at ease, more trusting of you, you can let them know you are *with* their perception (of their world) at the moment—without agreeing or disagreeing, without giving advice, evaluation, or blame. One of the better ways to do this is simply to repeat, restate, or reframe the talker's thoughts and ideas back using "new" words. That is, simply summarize the story and repeat it back, using new words and make the shortest statements possible. As noted, this takes skill and practice. Again, this response is most appropriately used in your personal relationships and/or when you are striking up new relationships.

In addition to the open-ended question and clarification/ summary responses, you can make a response that shows you are trying to tune in to the feeling(s) being revealed by the talker. As noted, as the person is speaking, think to yourself, is it pleasant, unpleasant or both for the other person right now. Then, "label" the feeling to yourself and reflect it (the feeling) back to the person who has just spoken—like a mirror. Again, reflect using new words and make short, to the point statements. As stressed previously, this response should *not* be made unless you are *genuinely* interested in empathically listening to, and tuning in to the feelings of, the other person. And, remember, this response may not be appropriate for use when communicating with participants from certain cultural groups. Most definitely, this response should be reserved for use in your *personal* relationships.

I wish to acknowledge (again) that there are obviously many and varied verbal responses not provided in this book that will also facilitate your communication with others. Those that were presented here have been researched and the evidence clearly indicates their respective facilitative value. I also wish to acknowledge (again) that you will, and should, continue to give timely advice, use the "why" question, and so forth. However, it has been suggested throughout this book that *decreasing* the frequency of using the less facilitative responses, while *increasing* the use of the higher facilitative responses, will increase your opportunities to communicate more effectively with individuals from different cultural groups as well as with those who are similar to you.

Outside Practice Activity

Listed below are six sample (hypothetical) interactions. You have two tasks for each situation provided. First, *identify the type of facilitative response* made by the person. Second, *write the alternative type of facilitative response specified*. Be prepared to discuss your responses with other members of your group/class.

Sample 1

Elizabeth: *I never realized I learned so much from Carlos. I really am impressed with his culture.*

James: *You're surprised.*

Type of response given: _____

Your *open-ended question response* (begin your question with how, when, where, or what): _____

_____

Sample 2

Jennifer: *My resume shows that I should be an excellent accountant. You think the fact that I'm Black is why no one is hiring me.*

Jim: *It always takes a long time to get your first job.*

Type of response given: _____

Your *clarifying and summarizing response* (restate the content in fresh words and keep it short): _____

_____

Sample 3

Carlos: *I'm really having a tough time coping with my Black friend's activism.*

Dave: *You need to loosen up, there's nothing wrong with the Black Pride Movement.*

Type of response given: _____

Your *open-ended question response* (begin your question with what, how, when, or where): _____

_____

Sample 4

Linda (to her Anglo friend): *Mind your own business! You don't know how Hispanic's think!*

Sister: *You're angry because you didn't want to hear the truth.*

Type of response given: _____

Your *tuning in to feeling response* (think about how Linda must be feeling and reflect it back without a "because"): _____

_____

SAMPLE 5

Ling (to his supervisor): *What do you mean when you say I can't do that?*

Supervisor: *You should have listened to me; then you'd know what I mean.*

Type of response given: _____

Your *clarifying and summarizing response* (repeat or rephrase the content in fresh words): _____

_____

Sample 6

Aaron: "When Janice gets in one of those moods I can't figure out whether or not she likes me."

Mary: *You should talk to her about that.*

Type of response given: _____

Your *tuning in to feeling response* (What is Aaron feeling? Guess and mirror it back to him without any evaluation or judgment on your part): _____

_____

Group Practice Activity

Instructor's Note:

Read the following fantasy aloud to the participants. Then place them into groups of 5 or 6 and request that they take turns sharing their respective fantasies. Suggest that they use the high facilitative responses only (tuning in to feelings, clarifying / summarizing, and/or open-ended questions (what, how, when, or where) during their discussion. Specifically request that they not "interpret" another's fantasy. However, self interpretation may be appropriate.

A Structured Fantasy

"You're feeling relaxed now; you're very calm; it's in the middle of the week, just prior to bed time. You find yourself sitting in your comfortable chair very relaxed. Your eyes are closing.... You are tired, very tired, and decide to go to bed. You enter a very restful sleep, a very restful sleep; it's just one of those nights when you feel very good, very sleepy, very restful (pause 15 seconds). Now, visualize yourself awakening the next morning. You see yourself entering your bathroom; now, take a careful look in the mirror; you see there's been a rather startling transformation during the night.... You woke up as a member of another culture with physical characteristics typical of those from that culture.... You went to bed as a member of one culture and you woke up a member of another! (pause). How does it feel? (pause) What are your thoughts as you look at yourself there in the mirror? (pause) Now, you find yourself walking outside and meeting your best friend. How does your friend react? (pause) Now, visualize yourself walking across the campus; how do people react to you? You meet your favorite teacher—what happens? How do you feel? What is the overall reaction towards you? (pause) OK. Open your eyes now.

Group Practice Activity

Inter-Racial Communication

This activity will assist different cultural and/or racial groups to understand and respect their similarities and differences.

Instructor's Note:

This exercise is written using African Americans and Hispanic Americans as an example only. Any homogenous groups can participate.

Begin this activity with homogenous groupings by race (6-7 African Americans at a table and 6-7 Hispanic Americans at separate tables). Each African-American and Hispanic-American group is given a piece of newsprint and given the following assignment:

"African Americans, what is it that Hispanic Americans do, in general, that causes the communication breakdown between the two races?" (on campus, at this school, and so forth.)

And then, turning to the Hispanic Americans:

"Hispanics, what is it that African Americans do, in general, that is causing the communication breakdown between the races?"

Next, ask each table to list (large enough to be read across the room) eight to ten points (no personal names) on the newsprint using a large black felt tipped pen. When each table finishes their assignment, provide each with a new piece of newsprint and a red felt tipped pen and give the following (surprise) assignment:

"What did the other groups write about you?"

Then, after they completed this second part of the assignment, bring the participants together into a heterogeneous circle (with their respective newsprints) to a "new" group setting and facilitate the discussion. (**Caution:** Do not let this develop into an argumentative, judgmental, blaming type activity. Use the facilitative model of communication—open-ended questions, clarification, and tuning in to feelings responses).

Did the respective groups know (quite accurately) what the "other" group wrote about them? Usually we know what is causing our interpersonal communication problems with others; we simply have not discussed our differences in a facilitative manner with one another.

Outside Practice Activity

Remember Carlos and Priscilla? Now you have the opportunity to respond to them again.

Example 1:

Assume you are talking with a friend, Priscilla, who is culturally different from you and attending college (while living at home). You want to know about her vocational interests and future plans. Priscilla says to you, "I'm really interested in going to graduate school to study interior design, but there are none close by. I don't want to leave home and go away to college just yet." How would you respond in this situation? What would be your first response (words) to her?

You want to communicate as facilitatively as possible. Several possible responses are listed below. Rank order them (in your opinion) from most facilitative to least facilitative. Place a 1 beside your most facilitative response, a 2 beside your next most facilitative response, and so on to 7, the least facilitative response.

_____ a. You shouldn't be afraid to go away from home to graduate school. That may just be your culture. It's time for you to leave home and it would be good for you.

_____ b. What is it about leaving home that concerns you most?

_____ c. You're concerned about being away from your family.

_____ d. Going away could be fun and you'll probably enjoy it after awhile.

_____ e. Right now you don't want to leave your family and go away to graduate school.

_____ f. Don't you like living away from home?

_____ g. You don't want to leave home because you've never been away from your family before.

Now, let us try again. Your goal is to make a facilitative statement to a friend—a statement that will be perceived as facilitative and helpful. Read over the possible responses below and again rank order them from one to six, from 1 for that response you consider to be the most understanding and facilitative to 7, the one you consider least facilitative. Look at your responses again. Do you see how the higher facilitative responses might improve communication?

Example 2:

Carlos, your roommate, returns to school from a weekend at home and says he wishes he had a home like others. He reports, sadly, that his parents fight a lot. He doesn't know what to do. He has heard his parents arguing and worries that his father may leave home and not come back. And, their arguing is really affecting his school work.

_____ a. What do you do when you hear your parents arguing?

_____ b. Hearing your parents argue frightens you and its having a negative impact on your studies.

_____ c. Hearing your parents argue makes you realize how dependent you are on them, and you're wondering just how much they do care for you.

_____ d. Try to get more involved in your schoolwork and don't go home so often. It might help to take your mind off the problems at home, and you'll feel better.

_____ e. There's nothing wrong with parents getting upset with one another, or your being concerned. I'd probably feel the way you do too.

_____ f. You're thinking that your family is not like other families in that they fight more than most.

_____ g. Do they argue all the time?

As before, check your rankings with my rankings below. How do yours compare? If you are within one or two numbers of my rankings, respectively, give yourself credit—you are learning the facilitative skills! Good luck as you work toward becoming an "everyday" facilitator of others!

My Rankings

Example 1:

a. 7; b. 3; c. 1; d. 5; e. 2; f. 4 g. 6

Example 2:

a. 3; b. 1; c. 6; d. 7; e. 5; f. 2 g. 4

Epilogue

Chapter XII

Facilitative Communication:

The End of the Beginning

Mary Howard-Hamilton, Ed.D.

Chapter *XII*

Facilitative Communication: The End of the Beginning

by Mary Howard-Hamilton, Ed.D.

Mary Howard-Hamilton, Ed.D., is an Assistant Professor in the Counselor Education Department at the University of Florida. She received her Bachelor of Arts and Master of Arts degrees from the University of Iowa and her Doctor of Education degree from North Carolina State University. Dr. Howard-Hamilton has researched the matriculation and attrition rates of African-American college students and is also interested in gender role socialization research.

Since you have taken the time to read this book, you are most likely an individual particularly interested in learning how to better communicate with others, especially with those different from you. Furthermore, if you have read this book carefully, and experienced the end-of-chapter activities, you have gained *skills* which will assist you in becoming a more facilitative communicator with others regardless of your or their race, creed, culture, or religion. In addition, the *knowledge* gained by reading and understanding those chapters written by members of different cultural groups (chapters 5 through 8) will be invaluable in your attempt to better communicate with individual members of those specific groups. However, it is my opinion that this is only the beginning, as opposed to the end of this interesting knowledge-gaining and important skill-acquisition adventure! That is, learning to facilitatively communicate with those who are different, and to value their differences, is a continuous, life-long, ever-changing process. The latter seems especially applicable in a country such as ours which will become even more multiethnic in nature as the years go by.

Some Demographic Trends:

In previous chapters, Wittmer and other contributors to this book have given you a variety of important demographic data concerning different cultural groups found in the United States. However, it seems important to reiterate here that America is quickly becoming a truly multicultural society. Thus, understanding and valuing differences and similarities will become social "musts" by the mid-point of this decade. Several authors (Henry, 1990, Levine, 1990, Mitgang, 1991) pointed to significant facts and figures that will reshape the way we communicate and associate with one another in America. These writers noted that the following demographic changes can be expected to occur in our country by the year 2000:

1. Asian and Pacific Islanders, the fastest growing ethnic group, is calculated to grow to nearly ten million by the next millennium and will make up nearly 4 percent of the total population. Asian and Pacific Island college level enrollment will grow at a faster rate than any other ethnic group, climbing to nearly 900,000 by the year 2000, representing 7 percent of all students in higher education.

2. The overall African-American population will increase 16 percent and total 35 million individuals by the year 2000. Most of the growth will be in five states: 32 million in New York, 2.9 million in California, 2.4 million in Texas, 2.3 million in Florida, and 2.2 million in Georgia. African-American college students will be the second largest ethnic group by the year 2000.

3. Hispanic or Latino college level students will become the country's largest ethnic group, but concurrently will be highly educationally disadvantaged. Overall, the Latino population is estimated to increase 21 percent by the year 2000.

4. Overall, Native-Americans and Alaskan Natives will remain the smallest ethnic/racial group growing from 321,000 in 1985 to a projected 414,000 in 1994, which reflects approximately a 29 percent increase.

The aforementioned demographic trends are insightful and clearly point to the need for America's educational institutions to implement teaching or training techniques, like those outlined in this book, on communicating effectively with people of color. Unless we work at the process of valuing our differences, and, in communicating more effectively to bridge these differences, discrimination will only continue. As Roberts (1982) wrote:

"Discrimination based on race, color, and national origin has been with us for centuries. It remains with us now, despite these trends and a claim to being an enlightened society. Our language—with its power to reinforce bias and shape thought—is still stubbornly preserving that "Old World" culture as the standard against which all other groups are judged" (p. 4).

Our nation was established with an infusion of cultures, religions, traditions, and languages unlike any other country in the world. However, as we began our quest to become an international power, it was felt that the *homogenization* of our unique characteristics was a significant factor for success. By developing a monocultural and monolingual society, our values, views, and communication patterns become elitist even bordering on arrogance, a result making us one nation, indivisible, without any appreciation for diversity. If we continue to encourage this melting pot philosophy and stress, for example, that the "English" language should be the unifying communication tool in our society, we will continue to waste valuable cultural resources available to us (Melendez, 1991).

As stated previously by Wittmer, the melting pot philosophy perpetuates discrimination and exclusion. Moreover, this philosophy does not celebrate, tolerate, nor embrace the differences people of color bring with them as a result of their respective value systems. Under the melting pot myth, difference has been equated with deficient (Melendez, 1991), resulting in the people of color in America to suffer tremendously because of this mindset.

The debate over cultural communication styles has been brewing for the past two decades. For example, Patricia Ann Johnson (1974) stated that a myth exists regarding the poor verbal skills of African-American children. She suggested that there are varying degrees of differences between African-American verbal skills and white verbal style. But, this does not mean that the African-American child should be viewed as inferior; it means that the African-American experience produces unique verbal skills indigenous to ones own community or environment, and that these skills are not promoted, validated, or accepted in the traditional classroom. As Johnson (1974) stated, "Black children are not inarticulate. They simply are not permitted to bring their Black culture and verbal skills into the classroom; they are also forced to leave their cognitive learning and expressive styles at home" (p. 82.). This is but another example to be cited explaining the value for gaining cognitive knowledge about different cultural groups. As Wittmer stated, this is a necessary prerequisite to open effective communication with those who are "different."

When we talk about communication and language skills across cultures, we are dialoguing about the basic need to validate who we are. In other words, language conveys the experiences felt in our communities. I am not just referring to African-American communities, but to Latino, Asian-American, as well as Native-American communities. The languages expressed in these diverse communities cannot be melted, enmeshed, or interchanged because they do not express the same thoughts, emotions, or experiences across cultures. As Wittmer stated, the latter are "culturally determined." Thus, the languages, experiences, and communication styles of various cultures are not universal. Each style makes its own personal, social, and political statement and should be appreciated, valued, and preserved.

As Wittmer noted in Chapter 9, a culturally skilled communicator is aware of the assumptions, biases, and individual cultural values that are operating in one's environment. Additionally, a culturally skilled communicator values and acknowledges another person's worldview. Our society has traditionally placed a tremendous amount of value on "individual" achievement and the importance of "self" (Spence, 1983). Central to this ideology has been the perception of the world as a set of impersonal forces that human beings master and exploit for their own benefit (Spence, 1983). Unfortunately, there has not been a concerted effort to role-take or understand the perspective, worldview, or value system of participants from the non-dominant cultures in America. If society covertly and overtly endorses the belief that it is acceptable for those of a predominant culture or worldview to denigrate and exploit others who do not have the same perspective, endorsing the statement that "all men are created equal" is difficult at best. It takes hard work, skill, ingenuity, and intellectual prowess to prosper and achieve in this society. Yet, there are those who work hard and have skills but who, nonetheless, seldom satisfactorily achieve at levels indicative of success as measured by societal norms. Caring, compassionate, facilitative communicators, as described in this book, will be willing and able to recognize these societal deficits and employ care, justice, the valuing of diversity, and other forms of principled thinking into their day to day interactions with persons from cultures other than their own.

Bailey (1982) postulated that interpersonal *communication* provides the legs for bias, carrying it from person to person, from generation to generation. Eventually, however, this same vehicle—communication, will be the method by which, to one day, end discrimination (p. iii). Facilitative communicators, according to Wittmer, are aware of their own biases, values, and assumptions. In addition, he has presented several guidelines in this book that provide facilitative communicators with alternatives which recognize the broadening of racial and ethnic culture. Roberts (1982) added to these important guidelines:

1. Beware of words, images, and situations that imply that the majority of racial or ethnic groups "are all alike." Avoid the generalization that most African Americans are on welfare, or that most Native Americans are alcoholics, or that most Latinos are migrant workers.

2. Avoid qualifiers that support or reinforce racial and ethnic stereotypes, e.g., "Dr. Mary Jones, an intelligent African-American attorney, addressed the faculty last night."

   The aforementioned statement provides extra information or a qualifier suggesting that this person is an exception to the rule within the African-American culture.

3. Identify or recognize an individual by race or ethnic origin only when relevant. Roberts (1982) noted that inappropriate phrasing can be easily identified if the reader or writer substituted the word "white" when describing an individual. If the sentence seems awkward to the ear or eye, then the identification of an individual by her or his race is irrelevant. Roberts (1992, p. 10) used the following example to stress her point:

"John Jones, noted white mayor of ABC City...." Does this statement look/sound strange? If so, then this statement should not be used:

"Jim Smith, noted African-American mayor of DEF City...."

As a person of color, I have been in numerous situations in which a description of my qualifications included my race. A person should not be introduced or described by using his or her race or gender unless it is germane to the topic of a speech, workshop, or program. Another example, to emphasize the awkwardness of race in an introduction, would be as follows:

Dr. Joe Wittmer, an Amish descendent, author of *The Facilitative*...." Or, "Dr. Mary Howard-Hamilton, an African American, contributed to Wittmer's book on facilitative...."

4. Be aware of language that to some persons has questionable racially biased undertones. For example, as noted elsewhere in this book, the use of the words "culturally deprived," "disadvantaged," or "impoverished" to describe individuals from racial and ethnic groups, e.g. "The university is attempting to admit 100 students from culturally deprived backgrounds this fall." A statement such as this should be avoided in written and oral communication.

5. Avoid usage of color symbolic words such as, "black sheep," "black balled," or "yellow coward."

6. Avoid patronizing and tokenism toward racial or ethnic groups.

7. Replace substantive information for ethnic cliches, i.e., a person of Spanish heritage might prefer to be asked about family history or political experiences, rather than always being asked about fiestas (Roberts, 1982, p. 15).

8. Scrutinize journals, publications, and other forms of media to see if all groups are fairly represented before using them.

As you have been asked throughout this book, are you aware of your own values and biases and how they affect those culturally different from you? It is important that as "everyday facilitators" we be the impetus for non-discriminatory communication. Modeling the eight objectives for nondiscriminatory ethnic and racial communication, as well as others noted elsewhere in this book, is definitely a step in the right direction.

Summary

One of the basic tenets of this book is that rather than homogenize our various communication styles, we should celebrate and embrace the differences and similarities. However, the focus is more on pluralism, or the fact that many distinct and unique entities exist in our society. As opposed to the "melting pot," Wittmer referred to this as a "salad bowl." And, as Melendez (1991) posited, we might also compare our linguistic styles to a *symphony orchestra*. An orchestra has numerous instruments with varying pitches, tones, and sounds. However, with skill and practice each instrument can, and will, harmonize with one another and produce melodious music. Of course, sometimes dissonance can be heard among the instruments. A chord may be struck that is discordant or inharmonious, but the instruments still work together and end up on a chord that is a blend of their varying degrees of sounds. The symphony orchestra is like the heterogeneous cultures in our society; we have different backgrounds, beliefs, and ideologies but we can still support and nurture each other if our differences are valued. Much like a symphony orchestra, there will probably always be some dissonance, discord, or dissension among the various cultural groups found in America. But, by working and communicating together effectively, a balance can be found.

Communication is the key that could unlock the door to world peace and ultimately our survival as a country. I agree with the words of Paulo Freire (1989) who stated that the transformation of our society can only take place if there is a dialogue between and among individuals of varying cultures and reflection on the information shared by these individuals. In such interaction, if dialogue or reflection is sacrificed, intercultural communication truly suffers. It is my opinion that communication across cultures and unification can be viewed as synonymous terms. As Hernandez (1991) stated, "Unity is the completed puzzle, diversity the pieces of the puzzle. And until we recognize every piece, we cannot have true unity" (p. 19). To embellish Hernandez's statement, if we do not add interpersonal communication to help solve the puzzle, we will never experience true unity.

As Wittmer stated in the preface of this book, we are a nation of diverse populations and groups. There seems no doubt that the future of our society depends upon our ability to talk with one another and to reach mutual understanding regarding our differences and similarities. As we understand ourselves and others better, we gain more respect for others as well as personal regard.

Valuing diversity and appreciating similarities begins with understanding. It is always based on how open we are to learning about others and how aware and open we are to our own personal experiences, values, and beliefs. As Wittmer also stated in the preface, facilitating intercultural communication can be an <u>adventure</u>, one in which new friendships develop, learning occurs, and personal insights are frequent.

However, as was also written in the preface of this book, being a facilitative communicator is not a "gift" with which we are born. It involves skills that can be learned and an awareness and sensitivity toward others that can be developed. As noted, by reading this book you have taken the first step in the process of learning the skills and gaining the knowledge that will enhance your ability to communicate with others who may be different from you. Welcome to the beginning; however, do not let this be the end of your adventure!

References

Bailey, J.N. (1982). "Preface," in Pickens, J. C. (ed.), *Without bias: A guidebook for non-discriminatory communication,* 2nd ed. New York: Wiley, pp. iii-iv.

Freire, P. (1980). *Pedagogy of the oppressed.* New York: Continuum.

Henry, W.A. (1990, April 9). "Beyond the melting pot." *Time,* pp. 28-31.

Hernandez, A. (1991, July 8). "What do we have in common?" *Time,* p. 19.

Johnson, P.A. (1974, August). "Intellectual genocide." *Black World,* pp. 81-82.

Levine, A. & Associates (1990). *Shaping higher education's future: Demographic realities and opportunities 1900-2000.* San Francisco: Jossey-Bass.

Melendez, S.E. (1991, September). *Educational imperatives for the public good: Creating diversity on our nation's campuses.* Paper presented at the National Council of Educational Opportunities Association, Tampa Florida.

Mitgang, L. (1991, September 18). "By 1995 schools to be 34% minority." *Gainesville Sun,* pp 1A, 8A.

Roberts, L.C. (1982). Regardless of race: Toward communication free of racial and ethnic bias." In Pickens, J. C. (ed.), *Without Bias: A Guidebook for Non-Discriminatory Communication,* 2nd ed. New York: Wiley, pp. 4-22.

Spence, J.T. (1983). "Introduction," Spence, J. C. (ed.) *Achievement and achievement motives: Psychological and sociological approaches.* San Francisco: Freeman, pp. 1-5.